Learning Support for
Young People in
Transition

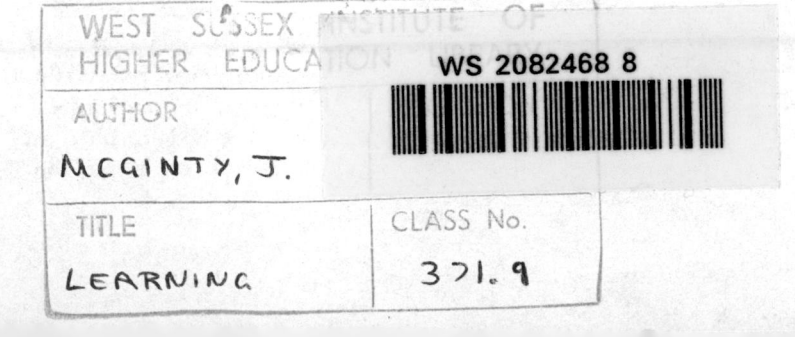

Open University Press
Children With Special Needs Series

Editors.
PHILLIP WILLIAMS
Emeritus Professor of Education
University College of North Wales, Bangor.
PETER YOUNG
Formerly Tutor in the education of children with
learning difficulties, Cambridge Institute of Education;
educational writer, researcher and consultant.

This is a series of short and authoritative introductions for parents, teachers, professionals and anyone concerned with children and young people with special needs. The series will cover the range of physical, sensory, mental emotional and behavioural difficulties, and the changing needs from infancy to adult life in the family, at school, in further education and in society. The authors have been selected for their wide experience and close professional involvement in their particular fields. All have written penetrating and practical books readily accessible to non-specialists.

TITLES IN THE SERIES

Learning Support for Young People in Transition

Leaving School for Further Education and Work

Jean McGinty and John Fish

Open University Press
Buckingham • Philadelphia

Open University Press
Celtic Court
22 Ballmoor
Buckingham
MK18 1XW

and
1900 Frost Road, Suite 101
Bristol, PA 19007, USA

First Published 1992

A catalogue record of this book is available from the British Library

Library of Congress Cataloging-in-Publication Data

McGinty, Jean, 1928–
    Learning support for young people in transition:leaving school for further
education and work/Jean McGinty, John Fish.
        p.   cm. – (Children with special needs)
    Includes bibliographical references (p.   ) and index.
    ISBN 0-335-09765-0
    1. Handicapped–Education–United States.   2. Vocational guidance for
the handicapped–United States.   3. Handicapped–Employment–United
States.   I. Fish, John.   II. Title.   III. Series.
LC4031.M4   1992
371.9–dc20   91–33757
                                                                      CIP

Typeset by Colset (Pte) Ltd, Singapore and London
Printed in Great Britain by Biddles Ltd, Guildford and King's Lynn

Contents

Series Editors' Introduction

Adolescence is a difficult period of transition by the very nature of human development: a growing-up which is at once a biochemical explosion and a change from dependency to responsibility when decisions have to be made which sometimes seem to be irrevocable. It is always difficult to respond to the tyranny of choice; yet, in adolescence, choices have to be made about the subjects to be studied, the courses to be taken, the training and qualifications to be gained, the career to follow, whether to work for others or for oneself. Decisions must be made, too, about the advice offered by parents, teachers, one's peers and advisers from a variety of agencies. Often there is one gulf between what young people would wish to do and what they are capable of doing and another gulf between what they are capable of doing and the opportunities open to them.

When society is in transition and the future is uncertain, the problems of making decisions are particularly difficult for adolescents. Unemployment and redundancies in the areas in which they live and in the industries, firms and institutions in which they hope ultimately to be employed may add to their difficulties. For young people with special needs all these factors make their transition to work a difficult and complex matter. Assessing their needs and potential, guiding them, preparing them and advising them is a matter which requires sensitivity and a detailed and realistic understanding of the opportunities which exist and the agencies which offer help and support.

Jean McGinty and John Fish address the subject of transition as a coherent whole. They treat it, not as a disjuncture, but as a continuity of the learning process. The process of service delivery, they argue, is essentially one of co-ordinating resources. Their book provides a detailed and insightful overview of the agencies, facilities and their functions against the background of recent legislation. What is particularly valuable is that they present a wealth of information in such a lucid and trenchant manner that one is constantly reminded not of the difficulties but of the opportunities and not of the shortfalls of legislation but of ways to improve it. Frequent check-lists and summaries add to the accessibility of all that they have to say.

Whether young people with disabilities are going straight from school to work or to training or are continuing in education preparatory to taking up a career, this book will provide many of the answers to the questions which will be uppermost in their minds and in the minds of their parents. For administrators, governors and professionals concerned with the education, training and vocational guidance of these young people this book is essential reading. And, in a society itself in transition, when market forces increasingly replace social service as the drive, this book should be read by legislators too.

Today, when these adults of tomorrow are moving out into the adult world of work there is no one agency, no one government department and a variety of voluntary bodies, all of which have their special roles to play. Departments of Health and Social Security, Education and Science, Employment, Trade and Industry are all involved but no one body deals with all the aspects of the handicapped young person's needs. Here lie opportunities for effective co-operation and interaction, for the removal of bureaucratic barriers and for flexibility. Jean McGinty and John Fish, from the wealth of their experience and in-depth knowledge of their subject recognize, too, the need young people have for advocates to speak for them and to guide them through the maze. Reading their survey of good practice and opportunities here and abroad, one can only wish that both their words and their positive spirit inspires all who work with these young people, for theirs is the advocacy those in transition really need.

Phillip Williams
Peter Young

Preface

This book springs from two sources. The first is the innovative work revealed by the study of transition made by the Centre for Educational Research and Innovation (CERI) of the Organisation for Economic Cooperation and Development (OECD). The second is the lack of understanding of transition from school to a working life in this country. The OECD/CERI study gave the authors opportunities to look at many different approaches and to see what young disabled people could achieve when their transition was well planned and supported. Many young people in this country are not having the opportunities to which they are entitled. Professionals who work with them have only a very hazy idea of what transition is about.

The book is an overview designed to help the individual, whatever his or her background, to see transition as a whole. Many of the elements of the process have been only sketched in and further reading and study is required about many of them.

Successful transition depends on inter-agency co-operation, collaboration and planning. Specialist and sector concerns result in a narrow focus. Individuals and agencies cannot on their own support effective transitions. Professionals working in education, social service, health, employment and voluntary organizations can make an effective contribution to transition only by working with other professionals, with parents and with the young people themselves.

This book attempts to outline a framework for transition within which professionals, administrators, parents and young people might fit their contributions.

A book concentrating on transition from school to an adult working life cannot give enough attention to a number of background factors and conditions which may have an important influence on the phase and process. For example, equal opportunity issues of race and gender have not been examined although they affect individual opportunities.

While the book was being produced Government White Papers outlined major proposals for changes in the further and higher education system. Consultation was taking place and the future was uncertain. Change and development are inevitable. However, improved opportunities for young people with disabilities and learning difficulties are by no means certain. Indeed it may become more difficult to provide an adequate range of opportunities and coherent post-school programmes for these young people. However, if the importance of the process of transition is recognized post-school opportunities may continue to improve.

Parents and the family have a profound and lasting contribution to make to the adult life of young people, particularly those with special needs. Parenting through transition is a complex process deserving a separate book. Only limited space has been devoted to the needs of parents.

Finally, a major thesis is the development of a young person's responsibility for his or her own transition. The emphasis placed on professionals and services is an attempt to create the right conditions in which young people can make choices. But, in consequence, there is little specific to their needs.

The book is arranged in three parts:

- Part I includes the first three chapters, which sketch in the contextual background in which young people, their families and their educators are functioning and defines the nature of transition.
- Part II looks at its starting points, the final school years, the contribution of further education and training in the middle stage of transition and entry to work and independent living.
- Part III gives examples of interesting practices; discusses the major issues that should be addressed by transitional arrangements, management and staff development; and looks at issues facing all concerned with transition in the years ahead.

This book is not a blueprint but a basis for planning and development. The authors have relied on many sources of information and inspiration. They are too many to acknowledge individually. While accepting responsibility for the book the authors would like to thank all of those with whom they have worked on this theme.

List of Abbreviations

AE	Adult Education
BSI	British Standards in Industry
CBI	Confederation of British Industry
CERI	Centre for Educational Research and Innovation (a division of OECD)
DE	Department of Employment
DES	Department of Education and Science
DRO	Disablement Resettlement Officer
DSS	Department of Social Security
EBD	Emotional and Behaviour Difficulties
EMFEC	East Midlands Further Education Council
ERA	Education Reform Act 1988
FE	Further Education
FEU	Further Education Unit
GCSE	General Certificate of Secondary Education
HMI	Her Majesty's Inspectorate
HMSO	Her Majesty's Stationery Office
IEP	Individual Education Plan
ITR	Individual Transition Plan
ILEA	Inner London Education Authority
LDs	Learning Difficulties
MLDs	Modern Learning Difficulties
SLDs	Severe Learning Difficulties
SpLDs	Specific Learning Difficulties
LEA	Local Education Authority

LMS	Local Management of Schools
LMSS	Local Management of Special Schools
LMC	Local Management of Colleges
MENCAP	Royal Society for Mentally Handicapped Children and Adults
NHS	National Health Service
NVQ	National Vocational Qualifications
NROVA	National Record of Vocational Achievement
OECD	Organization for Economic Co-operation and Development
RNIB	Royal National Institute for the Blind
SEAC	Secondary Education Accreditation Council
SEN	Special Educational Needs
SKILL	National Bureau for Students with Disabilities
TA	Training Agency
TEC	Training and Enterprise Council
TEED	Training, Education and Enterprise Directorate
TUC	Trades Union Council
TVEI	Training and Vocational Education Initiative

PART I

CHAPTER 1

After School?

What are you going to do when you leave school? Adults often ask this question. Young people with significant disabilities and learning difficulties, however, are not often asked about their aspirations. Many people avoid discussing the future of children with complex special educational needs.

The opportunity to be educated has not always been offered to these young people. Dependent care and trivial activity was once seen as the only future for many of them. Even now, when children of school age are entitled to education there is no guarantee of post-school opportunities.

Pioneers have shown that young people with severe disabilities can achieve high levels of competence. Many individuals live independently and hold down a job, thus becoming contributors to society. But there is still ignorance and uncertainty about what is possible after school.

Opportunities and expectations remain generally limited. But times are changing. Opportunities in further education are increasing. Employment is now a real possibility for the majority if they receive appropriate education, training and support. This book is about the rights of all young people with disabilities and learning difficulties to an adult life with the same opportunities as their contemporaries.

It shows how transition can be made effective through the provision of appropriate facilities and services. The book draws on the experiences of other countries but concentrates on issues in the United Kingdom. The focus on special needs is not a different or separate focus. Attention to them during transition merely highlights issues common to all and has relevance for all young people leaving school and to other transitions they may make.

Parents and families can facilitate or inhibit the process of becoming an adult. A wide range of different professionals may make positive or negative contributions to the process. Finally, although administrators may define official categories of handicap, determine which young people are described as handicapped and decide what help they get to make an effective transition, it is young people themselves who should decide how they wish to prepare for their futures.

Young people, their families, professionals and administrators are the four groups whose interests and contributions will be addressed in this book. The context in which young people are having to make a transition will be discussed, with particular reference to the wide range of statutory and voluntary agencies involved.

Why This Book?

There are a number of reasons why a book of this kind may be helpful at the present time. Changing legislation, new attitudes to disability and changes in patterns of family life are some of them. New demographic patterns in the population, illustrated by smaller youth groups, are also affecting the labour market.

There are now greater possibilities of employment for disadvantaged groups including disabled young people leaving school. However, the main reason for writing it is different: it is to emphasize the importance of transition from school to an adult working life and to stress the need for support, continuity and coherence in that process.

Many contributors to transition in education, health and social services and voluntary organizations currently work in isolation from each other. Continuity between phases of education and between child and adult health services is limited and the effective co-ordination of effort between the different sectors of national and local government concerned is very hard to find. Above all young people and their families face a lack of coherent information, uncertain choices – which vary according to where they live – and little certainty about their entitlement to education, training and support as they leave school. A recent report by HMI (HMSO, 24/91/NS) gives a picture of unsatisfactory arrangements for many young people. This is not always due to a lack of resources but much more the result of limited understanding and inadequate planning for transition.

The Power of Old Messages

It takes a long time to change attitudes and the beliefs of older generations persist. Although there are many examples of individuals who successfully overcome disabilities, negative notions of disability and handicap are still common in the general population. A protective, charitable attitude to 'the handicapped' persists.

This book challenges old messages and looks at the opportunities available to school leavers in further education, vocational preparation and employment. The fact that one can now ask a question about 'after school?' for young people with disabilities and learning difficulties shows that some progress has been made. Pioneer educators, and the young people themselves have demonstrated that severe physical, sensory and intellectual disabilities are no bar to high educational standards, recognized qualifications and employment.

What is Expected of the Young People Concerned?

About five years ago one of the authors was concerned with a study of policies and practices for young people with disabilities in three member countries of the Organization for Economic Co-operation and Development (OECD, 1987). Making comparisons was very difficult because educational and social systems were different as were definitions of disability and handicap. One minor way of making comparisons was to look at what happened to children and young people with Down's syndrome.

In one country this condition was classified as a mental handicap and dealt with by a service with its own separate schools and vocational and day centres. Once labelled the track for the individual was clear. Although social integration was an objective of the mental handicap service, integrated education and open employment were seldom envisaged. In another country education and training was provided in separate schools and centres run by medical and psychological services with again only limited opportunities to live and learn outside separate provision.

Only in the third was the approach more individual with some young people with the disability in regular schools and some prepared for work. But the two colleagues involved in the study came from countries where a label did not define a future. In both of their countries there were programmes and supporting arrangements which enabled many young people with Down's syndrome to be educated in regular schools and to obtain and remain in open employment.

Opportunities for young people vary from country to country. There is a similar range of opportunities, or lack of them in this country. Much of the variation is based on tradition and expectation and where you live (MENCAP, 1989). Often there is little appreciation of what disabled young people can achieve and more importantly little attention to their own wishes and ambitions. Low expectations often result from ignorance, prejudice and fear of the unknown.

What is Transition?

Individuals experience many transitions on their way through life. Entering school and transferring to secondary school are two of them. The most important transition is probably that from childhood to adulthood. This one, on which this book concentrates, covers the period of life from the early teens to the middle twenties. It is both a time phase and a process:

- It is a *phase* or period of time between the teens and twenties which is broken up educationally and administratively. During the phase there are changes of responsibility from child to adult services, from school to further and higher education and from childhood dependence to adult responsibility.
- It is a *process* by which the individual grows through adolescence to adulthood and achieves the balanced state of dependence and independence which a particular community expects of its adult members.

Both the phase aspect and the process can be helped or hindered by the interventions of all the services and agencies who can, or do, make a contribution as well as by families.

In the past transition was a haphazard and unco-ordinated process left largely to uninformed young people and their families. When the flow of young people, without any training or preparation, from school to work was interrupted by youth unemployment something had to be done. Transition from school to an adult working life became a focus of attention in most developed countries mainly because of high levels of youth unemployment. A wide range of youth training and employment preparation schemes has been introduced to reduce unemployment and provide a more skilled and flexible work force. Gradually access to these training schemes has been extended to young people with disabilities.

Transition for young people with disabilities and significant learning difficulties is a more complex process than for their contemporaries. It was pressure for equal opportunities from disabled young people and from the voluntary organizations representing their interests together with an increased recognition of their basic human rights that resulted in their inclusion in programmes.

A second reason for attention to transition has been the social and economic cost of life-long dependency. An independent adult life in employment is seen as an important way to reduce this cost.

Transition to adult and working life has been the subject of study by CERI of OECD since the late seventies (OECD, 1986). At first it was thought that alternatives to paid employment should be sought. However, the demand from individuals for equal opportunities and raised expectations led to an acceptance that the transition goals for young people with disabilities should be the same as those of their age groups.

Transition is a process, starting in school, which young people and their families share with nearly all national and local government departments and many voluntary agencies. For any young person to move successfully from school to work, and from one part of the system to another, requires careful planning, preparation, support and guidance. Ignoring this need can result in wasted effort on the part of professionals and disillusionment on the part of young people.

What is Adulthood?

In developed societies there is no clear initiation into adulthood (OECD, 1988). Although it is essentially a process of personal development, there are nevertheless a wide variety of legal and social indicators of adult status. Legal factors include defined ages for voting, service in the armed forces, financial responsibility, driving, marriage and assuming family responsibilities.

Obtaining work and earning money are powerful social indicators of an adult status as they enable individuals to break away from families and establish separate life styles and independence. Adulthood may be hard to define but the majority of young people strive to achieve that status and their families generally encourage the process.

Things are not so easy for young people with disabilities and significant learning difficulties, especially those who require regular physical care. It is not always evident that they are expected to be adults. Many more barriers to an adult life are placed in the path of these young people than their contemporaries through ignorance, prejudice and well-intentioned overprotection. Not all professionals, administrators and parents believe independence to be possible. Grateful dependence is easier to manage and it can be argued that there is a 'disability industry' with a vested interest in the continued dependence of those who are disabled.

Growing up in the 1990s

The context in which young people are living is subject to a number of major influences in the 1990s. Global concerns such as the ecology of the planet, population growth and global warming may be expected to influence daily life. They may affect energy use, transport, nutrition and patterns of employment and thus education and preparation for adulthood. European concerns, such as the major political changes in eastern Europe and the introduction of further stages in the development of the Common Market in 1992, will have their effect. Young people will expect to be prepared for living in the wider context of Europe.

The changing national context is no less important. New legislation in education, social security, health and social services is changing the context in which young people are growing up. An obsession with market forces together with a change from rights to means-tested entitlements is creating a different climate for minorities.

These contextual influences on professional practices, and on the options available, will have a significant influence on opportunities for young people with special needs of all kinds. In planning for transition it is as important to be sensitive to global, regional and national trends as to more local influences.

What are Special Needs?

Individuals with disabilities and learning difficulties have a wide variety of needs which vary from situation to situation (FEU, 1989b). The transition phase is one in which the nature of the needs change and special needs and handicap are redefined. It is therefore important to make clear the approach adopted here.

Figure 1 may illustrate the issues more clearly. It indicates the many relationships and interactions between disposing factors, disabilities and situations which result in an individual's difficulties. It also shows that there are only a limited number of modifications which can be made to meet them.

A variety of factors – column 1 includes some of them – give rise to disabilities and learning difficulties. The disabilities and difficulties which arise from these factors are described in a number of ways. Column 2 represents a common set of descriptions used in education and elsewhere.

Although physical and sensory disabilities and many severe intellectual disabilities are the result of genetic influences and illnesses there is no clear-cut difference between genetic and socially determined problems. The incidence of disabilities and difficulties may, however, be higher in

Figure 1

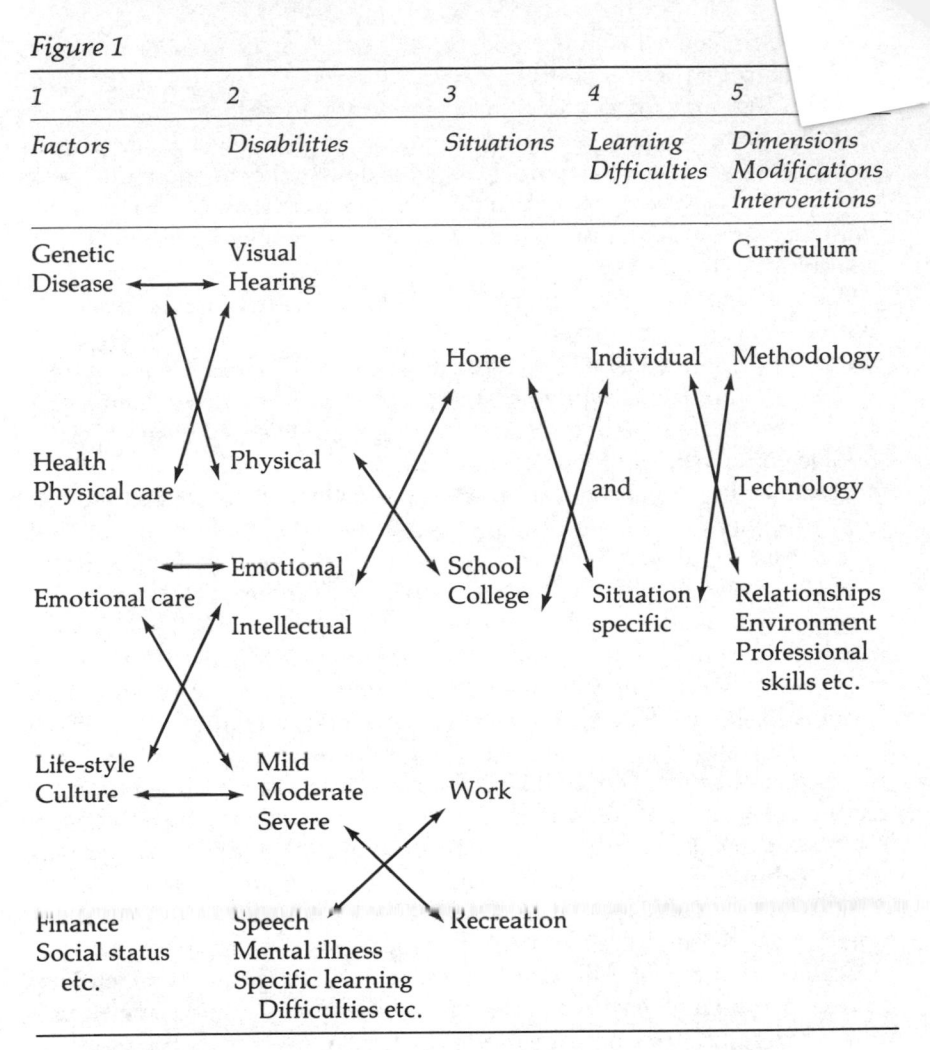

1	2	3	4	5
Factors	Disabilities	Situations	Learning Difficulties	Dimensions Modifications Interventions

families with an impoverished, low-status life style. Similarly, although many moderate learning difficulties and behaviour difficulties may be primarily due to life style, social status, finance and culture, genetic, disease and health factors play their part.

Any attempt to see special educational needs as broadly divided into those with a physical causation and those with a social causation over-simplifies a complex multi-factor background to most presenting disabilities. All the factors contribute to some extent to all the disabilities or difficulties.

Disabilities give rise to learning difficulties but again there is no simple relationship between a particular disability and the nature of the difficulties which may arise. Individuals with visual disabilities, for example, may also have a variety of other learning disabilities. Indeed, administrative decisions and not disabilities may decide whether an individual who is blind and has severe learning difficulties is placed in a school or class for children with visual disabilities or a school or class for intellectual disabilities.

A wide variety of voluntary organizations represent different disability interests. Each often presents a very simple relationship between a disability and the provision necessary to meet it. Organizations compete with each other for recognition, status and money, often by diminishing the common needs and exaggerating the special requirements of individuals with particular kinds of disabilities.

Specialist knowledge and skills are vital for the education and support of people with a particular disability but those individuals are not always best served by a large number of separate facilities and services based exclusively on narrowly defined categories of disability.

Learning difficulties which arise may also depend on the environment in which the individual is functioning (column 3). Home may present fewer learning difficulties than a strange house. School may reveal more learning problems than work or recreation. This is an important aspect in transition as young people move from one environment to another. Each of those environments may be more or less handicapping. Many factors contribute to an individual's learning difficulties (column 4), which vary from time to time and situation to situation. Meeting special needs involves both understanding the kinds of learning problems which may arise from particular disabilities and understanding and modifying situations to reduce those difficulties and eradicate unnecessary ones.

Column 5 in Figure 1 illustrates some of the modifications which may be necessary. They may be seen as characteristics of situations which face all young people during transition which may need to be modified to varying degrees in individual cases to enable effective learning to take place (Fish, 1989).

Conclusion

The focus of this book is the transition of young people with disabilities and learning difficulties to an adult working life. Themes have been introduced which will recur throughout the text. The transitional needs of these young people are not different in kind from those of their contemporaries and many of the issues are relevant to all young people leaving school.

CHAPTER 2

Towards Adulthood

The period from the early teens to the middle twenties is often one of confusion and uncertainty even for young people without obvious disadvantages. Social groups break up and reform as young people finish compulsory education and enter one of a variety of education, training and employment options. Aspirations and reality have to be reconciled. A pattern of adult life has to be initiated through informal learning in peer groups and testing out personal qualities in new situations. This transition phase and process requires a conceptual framework. Parameters need to be identified and questions such as 'what should be the aims of transition?' addressed.

If a young person has a disability or significant learning difficulty, professional and parental expectations of adult life may be uncertain and opportunities may be limited. Physical and psychological care since childhood may blunt an individual's drive to independence and reduce his or her expectations. Opportunities for informal learning with contemporaries and testing out behaviours may be much more limited either because they are more difficult to arrange or because of the psychological effects of long-term dependence on physical care. Positive and planned efforts are needed, in all areas of life, if an 'eternal childhood' is to be avoided and a reasonable quality of adult life achieved (Open University, 1986).

Achieving Adult Status

The overall aim of transition for young people is to achieve adult status. This is not clearly defined in complex societies (OECD, 1988). It is defined legally in terms of responsibilities and socially by access to certain institutions and groups. During the transition period young people themselves are often the strictest interpreters of status.

Psychological adulthood is, however, almost impossible to define. Adult relationships always contain elements of childhood ones. But there is agreement about patterns of behaviour and degrees of responsibility which define an adult. We tend to recognize adult behaviour even when we cannot describe it precisely.

Young people with disabilities find achieving adult status difficult for a number of reasons. Social groups do not easily accept independent young people with disabilities and dependence is often preferred. For some individuals there are legal barriers which do not allow the exercise of adult responsibilities. Achieving psychological adulthood is also more difficult when young people have disabilities requiring physical care. The dependent care relationships formed with adults may stand in the way of independence and autonomy. There are therefore personal and social barriers to adult status.

Reducing the handicapping effects of disabilities is an essential part of preparation for transition. Access to further education, vocational training, work, social interaction, an independent life and, above all, being treated as an adult, all reduce these effects.

What is Transition?

The transition we are discussing covers the period of life from the early teens to the middle twenties. It is both a phase in time and a process of personal growth and development. Effective transition should result in the development of the skills and knowledge appropriate for open employment, for an independent life, for a self-chosen range of leisure and recreational pursuits and, above all, for social interaction, constructive self-advocacy and community participation. The achievement of these objectives may take longer for some individuals and some may require long-term support to sustain their achievement.

It is particularly important that limitations should not be placed on the choices and opportunities available to young people with disabilities, when they leave school and before they have had experiences of work and independent living. Professional and parental preconceptions about the effects of disabilities on adult life may limit expectations. Young people should receive education, training, real experiences and support for a sustained period before, if ever, options are closed. Not to do so may be creating additional handicaps to the quality of adult life.

A conceptual framework for transition must look beyond the existing pattern of facilities and services which often circumscribe what is offered to young people. The approach must change from a service-led model, where what is on offer is what exists, to a needs-led model, where resources are used to meet assessed need.

The framework should encompass the range of options it might be realistic to offer if the resources, currently available, were used in another way or in a less sector specific and competitive way. A more co-ordinated approach to agreed ends should result in a more effective use of resources.

Stages of Transition

It is useful to identify three main stages of transition which may cover different time spans depending on the needs of the individual, on the way education and vocational training are organized locally and on the cultures, values and contexts in which transition takes place:

1. The final years of compulsory school.
2. Further education and vocational preparation.
3. The early years of employment and independent living.

The OECD/CERI study (OECD, 1986) has suggested that goals should be set in four main areas:

1. Employment, useful work and valued activity.
2. Personal autonomy, independent living and adult status.
3. Social interaction, community participation, leisure and recreation.
4. Adult roles within the family including marriage.

Each of these areas represents one aspect of an adult life but effective transition requires an approach in which they are tackled through a single coherent individual transition plan.

Many different agencies will inevitably be involved in the support of children and young people who are disabled. Education, health, employment and social service departments together with the social security department and voluntary agencies all have some responsibilities but no one agency is clearly responsible. Each department has its own terminology and definitions of the client group it considers to be handicapped or to have special needs. There are few agreed criteria; and different descriptions of the same disability, for example mental handicap and severe learning difficulty, add to the confusion.

Services and agencies tend to work in isolation from each other. Different phases of education often go their own way in ignorance of what professional colleagues have been offering the same individuals before and after their contribution. If these young people are to be helped to grow to an effective adulthood all relevant agencies need to co-ordinate their efforts.

Collaboration and co-ordination is difficult and time consuming but may well result in long-term benefits. It is reasonable for young people and their families to expect that all concerned will be working towards the same ends. Without an agreed conceptual framework for transition this is unlikely.

Major Elements in Transition

Work is perhaps the most important indicator of adult status. It provides economic independence and status in the community for those with disabilities. It is often their only opportunity for regular social interaction outside the home.

At the time of the Warnock Report (HMSO, 1978), when youth unemployment was high, the concept of 'significant living without work' was outlined. However, this is no longer acceptable. Disabled people resent the discriminatory nature of such a suggestion. The economic need for as many productive adults as possible is another reason for rejecting this concept.

Studies have shown that sheltered work is seldom an effective preparation for the labour market. Examples of education and training combined with flexible employment opportunities, in this country and elsewhere, have proved that the vast majority of those with severe disabilities can be enabled to work. These opportunities, which include self-employment and working from home, have been considerably increased by information technology.

Open employment and supported open employment, either for individuals or small groups in enclaves, has proved to be possible and sustainable for a much higher percentage of young people and adults with severe disabilities than was thought the case when the programme of OECD/CERI activities began. Time-filling trivial activity, which is personally demeaning and handicapping, is no longer acceptable as an objective. The aim must now be employment for all.

Personal Autonomy

Personal autonomy for those who are disabled is not just a quality of life but a human right. The expectations of parents and professionals have a crucial influence on the personal development of the individual young person.

Do facilities and services offer individual programmes which:

- Provide relevant and realistic situations in which to experience and examine adult attitudes and behaviours?
- Result in young people being able to choose and to manage their own lives?
- Offer regular and planned interaction with non-disabled contemporaries?

The transition phase should involve a major reorientation of professional and parental attitudes, practices and relationships with disabled young people. This is vital if these young people are to achieve a positive self-concept and manage their own lives to the maximum extent. Self-presentation and self-advocacy are essential ingredients in transition programmes.

Social Interaction and Community Participation

This is the aspect of transition where many issues surrounding the concept of integration come to the fore. After the compulsory school period social groups reform as young people follow a variety of education and training options or enter employment. Integration becomes not just a matter of attending the same school as others but a matter of access to the same range of post-school opportunities and groups as others. The process of integration is also important for the preparation of non-disabled young people to accept and understand their contemporaries who are disabled.

Nevertheless, at the end of transition, whether a young person was educated or trained in separate or integrated programmes may be less important than whether he or she is equipped for living in the community, has confidence to interact with others and knows how to access and participate in neighbourhood activities. This is not a separate issue from that of employment since appropriate social relationships are often important in retaining a job.

Adult Roles within the Family

It is not unreasonable to portray many traditional professional and parental expectations for young people with severe disabilities as an 'eternal childhood'. Facilities and services have moved towards providing a 'normalized' pattern of life. Nowhere is this more evident than in the living arrangements which have followed deinstitutionalization. But adult patterns of relationships and living are not yet as widely accepted particularly for those with severe disabilities and they continue to be less easy to achieve.

In recent years human rights movements have questioned continued dependent status. Marriage and having a family are slowly becoming recognized as acceptable goals. A conceptual framework for transition has to embrace the adult family roles, and group living patterns in the culture, as legitimate objectives for young people with disabilities.

Aspects of Transition

There are two interrelated ways of looking at transition and to concentration on one to the exclusion of the other is unwise. One approach is to study the range and quality of the facilities and services in an area and the options and choices they afford to individuals. Is the transition process recognized? What further education and training opportunities are available? What financial arrangements support young people during transition?

The second, equally important approach, is to study the progress individuals make as they move from school to adult and working life. This approach is probably more common than studies of facilities and services. What are the performance criteria by which young people will be assessed for training and employment programmes? How is individual progress through a transition programme evaluated?

The following aspects should be considered. They are outlined at this point to flesh out the concept of transition. In Chapter 9 they become indicators of quality.

Information

What sort of information is available to young people and their families at each stage of transition? Because of the fragmentary nature of responsibilities and services it is very difficult for young people and their families to get clear and accurate information about all the options available to them and all the support to which they are entitled.

Assessment

What sort of assessment is made at the beginning and during transition, who contributes to it, how is assessment information used and what is the outcome? Does assessment in the final years of schooling include evaluating performance in real-life situations outside school?

In most systems there is an individual assessment process towards the end of the school period. The purpose of assessment and the use to which it is put is crucial. If assessment at the end of schooling is used to categorize and if school performance is used to decide what individuals can or cannot do in other situations the result may be to limit choices and increase handicaps.

Programme Balance

Do the young person's opportunities, experiences and training possibilities achieve a reasonable balance between preparation for work, for independence, for participation in the community and for an adult family life? A narrow professional conception of transition can result in a lack of balance in programmes of activities. Programmes may not give equal weight to all assessed individual needs or to all the major aspects of transition.

Continuity and Progression

How much do professionals working in different phases of transition know of each others' work? How much do they co-operate to ensure coherence and progression in what is offered? What steps are taken to ensure that there is a consistency and continuity in the programme, in approaches to learning and in expectations? Is there evidence of progression as the individual moves from one phase to another and one agency to another?

These are important questions as individuals move from school to further education and vocational preparation, from one agency to another and from one professional responsibility to another. Discontinuities are common.

How are Families Involved?

What is the nature of parental involvement in transition programmes? Professionals working with adolescents tend to concentrate their efforts on developing the independence of the young people with whom they work. They may inform parents about programmes but they do not always discuss and agree the objectives of programmes with parents.

How is Participation and Self-Advocacy Developed?

In moving from school to adult and working life are steps taken to develop choice, self-presentation skills and participation in decision making as an integral part of an individual's programme? An effective programme should enable young people to manage many areas of their lives.

Financial Management

Are resources for individuals with disabilities always channelled through professionals or managed by parents? This aspect of transition is crucial to the development of autonomy. Do young people gradually obtain control over their financial affairs as they complete transition?

How do Professional Practices Change?

Are professionals aware of the need to change and create a new pattern of relationships with young people and their parents? Growing independence and adult status require a greater equality in participation and decision making.

What are Professional and Service Priorities?

It is argued that individuals need a personal transition plan. Do professionals and services work towards individual plans or do they categorize and stereotype individuals and fit them into the courses or programmes that the agency wants to provide? Are facilities and services flexible and responsive to changing individual needs over time?

Coherence

Experience has shown that the specific skills required in particular jobs are often of considerably less importance than the social and life skills necessary to function effectively in a place of work and the mobility to get to and from work. Participation in the community together with access to recreational and leisure activities depends on managing one's own resources, particularly those derived from paid employment, as well as on social skills. An independent life in a family or appropriate social group requires the status of a contributor as well as competence in the other areas of adult life.

Many programmes still concentrate on one aspect of transition, employment or independent living, for example, in isolation from other programmes – assuming that other aspects of individual development will 'happen'. The individual cannot be neatly divided into his health, education, social welfare and employment parts although administrative arrangements are often based on this assumption.

While it is unrealistic to expect that divisions of administrative responsibility will not persist or have an acceptable rationale, it is possible to hope that responsibilities will be seen as shared and will be exercised towards agreed common ends. It is now clear that a continuous and co-ordinated programme which makes sense to the individual and which uses available resources effectively is the best way to achieve a successful transition.

Coherence in transitional arrangements requires joint planning and inter-professional and inter-agency collaboration at national, regional and local levels.

Partners in Transition

It is important to identify all those who have a contribution to make to transition in partnership with young people and their families. The nature of individual contributions will become clear in due course. There are more than fifteen different professionals with potential contributions in the education sector alone.

Although professions are grouped in sectors it is important that managers of different sectors work together and that professionals, both generalists and specialists, recognize that they are contributing to one individual transition plan and not a separate plan for each sector.

Education

In education the professionals involved might include:

- education officers for schools and further education;
- advisors and inspectors;
- teachers in secondary schools;
- careers teachers;
- special education teachers in secondary and special schools;
- lecturers in colleges and adult tutors;
- college student support and guidance staff;
- co-ordinators for special needs in colleges and adult education;
- the staff of independent colleges;
- careers officers and specialist careers officers;
- educational psychologists;
- educational social workers.

Social Services

In social services the professionals concerned might include:

- authority, area and team managers;
- the child or young person's social worker;
- team disability specialists for different disabilities;

- day-centre staff;
- residential social workers;
- occupational therapists.

Health Services

In the health sector those concerned might include:

- paediatricians and community paediatricians;
- psychiatrists;
- physiotherapists;
- speech therapists;
- occupational therapists;
- community mental handicap teams;
- community mental health teams.

Employment

In the employment sector those involved might include:

- employment office staff;
- disablement resettlement officers;
- the staff of TECs;
- employers;
- employees;
- the staff of independent training agencies.

Voluntary Organizations

In the voluntary sector potential contributors might include:

- parents groups;
- disability groups;
- national staff of a voluntary organization;
- local officers of voluntary organizations.

These are formidable lists of different workers to which others could be added in particular circumstances. It is little wonder that there is confusion and fragmentation. To co-ordinate contributions from all these different areas of work in the interests of individuals making a transition is a formidable undertaking.

Conclusions

The possibilities for individuals will vary according to where they live. Opportunities may be more limited and services more difficult and expensive to provide in rural areas. Education, training and experience in residence away from home does not always prepare individuals for an integrated return to the community. However, there are successful examples of weekly (Monday to Friday) residential provision to serve rural areas. These arrangements enable young people to keep their roots in the community without the stress of travelling for long periods each day.

High unemployment may also be seen as an adverse factor although the work in the USA (Wehman *et al.*, 1988; Sailor *et al.*, 1989), to be described later, shows that an effective supported employment programme is not unduly affected by high unemployment.

There is also a tendency to allow a perceived degree of disability to influence transition opportunities. Disabilities may range from mild, through moderate to very severe. Definitions vary from country to country and a person with a severe intellectual disability can be found in a day centre in one place and open employment in another. All should have a transition plan and only the outcome should determine the longer term degree of dependence and care that an individual may require.

A framework for transition has been set out. Major parameters of the process and potential contributors have been identified. We turn now to the context in which individuals are making their way from school to adulthood.

CHAPTER 3

New Laws and Influences

Young people are moving from school to an adult working life in a society which has changed radically in the last decade. New legislation has been an important influence, but perhaps as significant, has been new political attitudes and social policies. This chapter will look at some recent legislation and its possible effects on the transition of young people with disabilities and learning difficulties.

Since 1979 the government has introduced major legislative changes in education, health and social services and in the social security system. Employment training for a changing labour market has also been the subject of legislation and frequent change. Other initiatives have included the brief introduction of the community charge, reduced responsibilities for local authorities and increased responsibilities for individuals. The government has increased its powers of overall control while at the same time delegating responsibilities elsewhere. Responsibilities without adequate powers and resources have been delegated to governors and boards of individual institutions. It has introduced increased choice for some at a cost to others.

A Changing Society

Competition and personal aspirations have increasingly been used to motivate. Market forces and performance criteria are seen as the main way to achieve standards. Although these useful tools have revitalized many aspects of commerce and industry, their positive influence is most evident on skilled and effective citizens. Their application to those limited or impaired in their abilities has not always been positive. Successful competitors with high material standards often present an increasingly stark contrast to the quality of life of those who are unsuccessful.

The response of the competitive society to disability and special need is often characterized by 'telethon' charity. This emotive form of giving makes the donor feel good. While those with disabilities appreciate help they do not wish to be diminished objects of charity. Equal opportunity and entitlement do not stem from morally superior giving.

The age structure in the population of industrial countries has changed. People are living longer, families are having fewer children, traditional family patterns are changing. The result is a larger proportion of older people having longer periods of retirement and smaller youth groups entering the labour market. The costs of the universal benefit systems introduced in the 1950s and 1960s have increased to such an extent that developed countries, whatever their political philosophies, cannot afford them.

Reviews of expenditure and social priorities have become essential. New patterns of social protection in industrial societies are being developed. These patterns must encourage the employment and financial independence of as many people as possible. Investment in training and support for employment are the main messages of *Labour Market Policies for the 1990s* (OECD, 1990). Because markets are seldom responsive to minority interests this approach requires new attitudes to those who are disadvantaged involving strenuous efforts to enable them to become contributors to society.

Why Legislation?

One of the main justifications for government of any kind is to protect citizens not only from external dangers but from the worst excesses of the behaviour of their fellows. This protection is not to encourage passive dependence but to allow the individual with less competence and assurance to be an unexploited contributor to society. A major question to be addressed in the UK is whether recent legislation has created the conditions which make such contributions possible.

Two other countries take very opposite approaches to legislation. In the USA there is a strong trend towards civil rights legislation starting with race and gender and more recently in the Americans with Disabilities Act 1990 (President's Committee on Employment of People with Disabilities – Fact Sheet 1990) assuring the civil rights of disabled citizens.

The President's Committee monitors the effectiveness of all legislation and regulations as they relate to disabled individuals.

In Denmark there is no separate legislation in education, employment and elsewhere. Every Act is said to apply to all citizens and the needs of disabled people must be taken into account in general policies and practices.

Although there has been a Minister responsible for disability matters for some years in the UK, there has been little evidence in this country of a coherent policy towards disability or any co-ordination of practices across departments. Each piece of departmental legislation is seen as an independent action. Even within departments, as recent educational legislation has shown, a co-ordinated approach cannot be assumed. The only positive initiative is a very small unit charged with knowing what is going on. A stronger unit could provide a valuable centre from which to co-ordinate policies and practices as they affect those who are disabled.

Education Legislation

The Education Act (1981)

At the beginning of the 1980s legislation based on the Warnock Report was placed on the statute book. The Act was implemented in 1983. The 1981 Education Act moved away from categories of handicap to a concept of special educational need. Special educational needs were defined as learning difficulties.

These learning difficulties of all kinds had to be significantly greater than those of the majority of children of the same age or the result of disabilities which prevented the child from using the facilities available to the majority of children in the area. The Act made it clear that primary and secondary schools were responsible for meeting special educational needs, particularly the broad range of learning difficulties commonly found in the school population.

Parents were given much wider rights and responsibilities in relation to assessment and provision. For children with severe, complex and long-term special educational needs procedures for assessment and for making a Statement of needs and provision were specified in detail. Statements, which should be agreed by parents and reviewed annually, cover the school period up to the age of 18 + . However, if a young person leaves school at 16 and enters further education the provisions of the Statement do not apply.

Legislation was introduced without additional resources and without enthusiasm by the government of the day. The Department of Education and Science (DES) financed research into its implementation (Goacher *et al.*, 1988) but little else. Most local authorities supported the legislation and put significant resources into its introduction. The Act was intended to improve arrangements for all children with special educational needs, up to one in five, at some time in their school life, but the (DES) made it clear that it was only interested in children who were the subject of Statements – a small minority of those with special educational needs.

The Act called for the co-operation of health and social services in assessment procedures. It was envisaged that provision would include therapies provided by health authorities and family support by social services. Subsequent research (Goacher *et al.*, 1988) showed little joint action in practice. The DES did fund further dissemination of good interagency practices (Evans *et al.*, 1989) but during the school period a co-ordinated inter-agency approach to special educational needs is not easy to achieve.

Further and continuing education was omitted from the 1981 Act. Although a promise was made at the time to bring in separate legislation nothing was done. The Warnock Report's (HMSO, 1978) priority recommendations for post-school provision did not, however, go unheeded in the field. Support for developments came from individuals and organizations. As subsequent chapters will show much progress was made in the absence of official policy and departmental interest.

The Education Reform Act (1988)

This dealt with all aspects of education managed by local education authorities including schools, further, higher and adult education. Its aim was to raise standards in education. The means of doing so included the introduction of a national curriculum, national assessments at the ages of 7, 11, 14 and 16 and the use of agreed performance criteria in further education.

The Act also introduced the delegation of resources and responsibilities to managers of schools and governors of colleges and the reduction of the direct involvement of local education authorities in administration and provision. Local education authorities now have greater responsibilities for the standard of education and increased inspectorial responsibilities.

A national curriculum for all also implicitly recognizes the fact that meeting special educational needs is an integral part of an educational system. The delivery of the National Curriculum must ensure the same core of subjects is offered to all pupils between the ages of 5 and 16 years. A richer and wider range of educational experiences may now be offered to many children receiving special education.

The introduction of city colleges and grant maintained schools and the local management of maintained schools is intended to offer parents choice. There are no obvious safeguards to ensure that special educational needs are met within these schools.

The Act requires all children with special educational needs to follow the National Curriculum except where it is modified or disapplied in individual cases. The same standards will be applied to all pupils in all schools through testing and assessment.

However, with limited budgets, meeting special educational needs may not be considered an effective use of scarce resources or a significant contribution to raising school standards. Children with Statements must have new or amended Statements to set out the extent to which the individual is expected to follow the National Curriculum. Children whose special educational needs do not require a Statement may also have the National Curriculum disapplied for short periods of time under certain circumstances. Procedures for making Statements or disapplication are such that they will not be undertaken lightly.

School effectiveness will be judged on the overall assessment of results. To expect differently managed and resourced schools with widely different catchment areas, and with individual admission policies, to achieve comparable standards for pupils with a wide range of different styles and rates of learning may be unreasonable.

The effects of these changes are as yet uncertain. It is already possible to sense a reluctance on the part of primary and secondary schools to accept children who are the subject of Statements. Increased referrals for special schools may occur. When the National Curriculum is fully introduced the vast majority of pupils leaving school will be expected to have experienced the same range of educational opportunities and to have been assessed on the same criteria. Further education will be building on the National Curriculum and assessments at age 16.

Other Legislation

Disabled Persons (Services Consultation & Representation) Act (1986)

This Act has only been implemented in part. Sections 5 and 6 concerning the preparation of a plan on leaving school, and inter-agency co-operation to produce and put it into effect, were implemented in 1988. A Social Services Inspectorate report (Warburton, 1990) two years later was depressing. Little was being done in most areas studied.

The definition of disability used in the Act dates from 1948 and the terminology used is no longer acceptable to many. One result of the narrow definitions used is that only a small proportion of those who have had their special educational needs met in school will become a social service responsibility. The Act is expected to be helpful to those with severe physical, sensory and intellectual disabilities but less helpful to young people with moderate and slight degrees of need.

With the other demands on social services and restraints on resources it is not surprising that little progress has been made. However, the Act does recognize some aspects of planning for transition and for the advocacy of individual needs. Its limited implementation is a sign that neither the government nor local authorities have recognized the costs of not supporting effective transitional arrangements.

Social Security Act 1989

Over the past few years the government has been introducing new regulations for social security payments and more recently proposals for disability benefits. Not all changes have proved to be a positive encouragement to independence. The proposal for a disabled work allowance may facilitate entry into employment and offset some of the effects of the costs of being employed. Another new initiative is the system of allowances for disabled students resulting from new legislation on student loans and grants. These should make higher education more accessible. Changes are noted here rather than described. Anyone concerned with transition must study the benefit system carefully.

The Children Act 1989

This Act, implemented in late 1991, simplifies court procedures, increases and clarifies the concept of parental responsibility and introduces a category of children in need among whom children with disabilities are included. The 1948 definitions are again used to define disability.

Local authorities are to keep a register of disabled children. In another archaic confusion the legal definition of child in the Act is anyone below the age of 18. This does little for the self respect of teenagers. The Act stresses the need for 'preparing to leave care', and this recognition may be very helpful to the transition of children on disability registers. Disabled persons are also clearly seen to have an entitlement to a 'normal life' and this too will help forward planning for transition. Preparation is a shared responsibility to which education will be expected to contribute.

The National Health Service and Community Care Act 1990

The government's White Paper in 1989 and subsequent legislation sets out proposals for community care. The resourcing and management of care and the new responsibilities of local authorities to manage rather than provide will take a long time to come into effect. However, the general thrust is very much in keeping with the transitional objectives set out in this book. Again inter-agency planning and co-operation are at the heart of successful practice.

Employment Legislation Training and Training and Enterprise Councils

New proposals for Training Enterprise Councils and training credits are other major developments taking place which are discussed in later chapters.

Education Underrated

An OECD review of the labour market, *Labour Market Policies for the 1990's* (OECD, 1990), shows the UK to have the second smallest percentage of seventeen year olds in full- or part-time education, in 1987, of all OECD member countries. Percentages for the USA and Scandinavia are twice those of the UK. By 1990 the staying on rate had increased to 53 per cent. The 1991 White Papers give high percentages of young people in education and training after the age of sixteen but only just over half the age group continue in full time education.

The constant Conservative criticism of education since 1979, and the lack of government support for those engaged in it, has resulted in low morale. Under resourced and undervalued, sapped by a war on teacher organizations, education in this country is ill-prepared for the twenty-first century.

The government approach has been to attempt to standardize what is taught and introduce competition between schools through increased parental choice and delegated management, particularly at the secondary education stage. A national curriculum taught in differently valued competitive schools chosen by poorly informed parents is seen to be the means of raising overall standards. Further education institutions are given independence and expected to be responsive to local market trends.

The value of education is belatedly being recognized by all politicians. Employers and trade unions are aware how far the system has fallen behind European partners in preparation for employment and citizenship. There is much to be done to prepare children and young people for the Europe of the twenty-first century.

Standards

Political attention has turned to educational standards since the early 1980s and the debate and campaign which followed led to the 1988 Educational Reform Act. Criteria by which to judge the effectiveness of education of different kinds are necessary. They require careful selection. Academic standards necessary for higher education may not always be appropriate for those interested in technical and vocational preparation after leaving school.

Criteria need to include the quality of learning and not just its quantity. If standards of teaching and performance criteria are appropriate they should be applicable to all education including that for those with special educational needs. High standards are equally important in the field of special education. Exemption from standards may do a disservice to those with disabilities and learning difficulties. The inappropriate application of standards may result in a differentiation which devalues the achievements of those with learning difficulties. Low expectations may turn disabilities and difficulties into handicaps (Further Education Unit (FEU), 1987a; FEU/Pickup, 1988).

The importance of education for *all* up to the age of at least eighteen years must be recognized. Government and parents must support what employers and unions both understand to be essential: namely, the preparation of an educated work force capable of flexibility, decision making and co-operative working practices. But education is not just a question of vocational preparation for a future labour market.

If society is to work, if crime and drug abuse is to be reduced and if the country is to be pleasant to live in education must be aimed at informed adulthood, lifelong learning and concern for others as well as vocational proficiency.

PART II

CHAPTER 4

The Final School Years

Preparation for being an adult begins from birth and all transitions from that time onwards are part of that preparation. Transitions from home to school and from primary to secondary school are some of them. However, transition to an adult working life begins in earnest in the secondary school when longer term plans need to be made and where serious preparations begin.

This transition starts from a common base, education in school; but, after the age of 16, individuals take a variety of routes to an adult and working life. Some will follow an academic route through A levels in the sixth form or further education (FE) college to university, polytechnic or college of higher education. Others will follow a variety of technical and professional training courses in FE colleges and elsewhere. In the past a significant percentage of school leavers went directly into work but now there is a variety of employment training schemes between leaving school and entering employment.

The general thesis is that young people with disabilities and learning difficulties are entitled to the same range of opportunities as their contemporaries. Concentration on the route through professional and technical training and vocational preparation in the following chapters is not intended to diminish the importance of higher education for many of these young people.

It is now necessary for individuals to follow a National Curriculum. Transition may start from knowledge, experience and competences which are more standardized as a result of common attainment targets for all. Whether that Curriculum, as at present outlined, is an appropriate preparation for adult life is another question. Attention here will be concentrated on how the Curriculum is delivered rather than its content.

This chapter looks at the secondary school stage up to the age of 16 and considers some of the characteristics which individuals need to develop during that period if they are to be prepared adequately for adulthood. It also discusses the nature of the transition plans which should be developing during those years and inter-agency collaboration necessary to implement them.

Objectives for Education and Transition

The main objectives of transition, outlined in Chapter 2, are the same for all young people whether disabled or not. What needs to be questioned is whether the aims of the National Curriculum for all are compatible with the reality that faces young people after school.

Secondary schools should be preparing their pupils for all the choices that await them in the post-school period. That implies that a concentration on the skills and knowledge necessary for higher education may not be appropriate for a significant percentage of the population of a non-selective school. A broader and more relevant curriculum is not just special pleading on behalf of those with special needs.

It is also drawing attention to the needs of up to 40 per cent of the school population. The views of the Confederation of British Industry (CBI, 1989), set out later, mirror this concern. An essential characteristic of education should be the provision of equal opportunities for all in terms of race, gender and disability. This aim should be expressed through the curriculum and its delivery.

Although it is legitimate to base predictions of success in higher education on performance in school, achievement in school is not necessarily a good predictor of the potential living and working proficiency of the majority of young people. For young people with special needs it is important that the possibility to enter employment and live independently should not be jeopardized in the final years of school by negative attitudes to disability, by low expectations and by a narrow academic curriculum.

Some of the qualities of adult life which should begin to be evident as a result of appropriate secondary education may be identified. Young people, including those with disabilities and learning difficulties, should be recognized as individuals, capable of growth and development, who are treated with dignity. They should be empowered to make their own choices. Every opportunity should be afforded to enable them to participate in the economic and social life of the community.

The Starting Point

It is assumed that the first serious preparation for transition will occur during the third secondary school year at 13 + years. This has traditionally been the time when choices are made in secondary schools.

It is now recognized that there is insufficient time in the school year to take all subjects of the National Curriculum to a reasonable level of competence at age 16. Choices will need to be made at this point for the final two years. Another reason for choosing 13 + as a starting point is that individuals are likely to be attending the schools in which they will complete their secondary education. Where there is a middle school system or where private education is chosen 13 + is the age when the final stages of compulsory secondary education begin and a sustained assault on GCSE begins. It is also the time when programmes such as the Training and Vocational Education Initiative (TVEI) begin and when careers education is becoming more significant. Finally, it is at this stage that the Education Act 1981 requires attention to review and reassessment for pupils with Statements. The process of reassessment for a future programme should begin and should result in a comprehensive transition plan.

Does the Starting Point Matter?

A number of questions need to be addressed at this point, the answers to which often indicate attitudes and expectations. Among them are:

- Where will pupils with special educational needs be in the system at the start of the transition plan?
- Will where they are being educated affect their transition?
- Will the National Curriculum be appropriate for them?
- Will the nature of their disabilities or difficulties prejudice their transition?

Which Secondary School?

Where children are educated has very clear social implications in the UK. The schools individuals attend influence other people's judgements of their future prospects. The marketing of secondary schools may be expected greatly to increase the effects of the school attended on individual prospects in the next decade.

When the 1988 Act was implemented almost all pupils with the wider range of special educational needs, not requiring a Statement, were being educated in comprehensive secondary schools. A majority of pupils with Statements were being educated in special schools while an increasing minority were receiving education in special units or regular classes in secondary schools.

The introduction of city technical colleges and grant-maintained secondary schools, together with the autonomy given to maintained secondary schools and increased parental choice, is expected to influence where special needs are met in future. How special educational needs are regarded, and particularly where pupils with needs, which are not considered to merit a Statement, are educated will become much less clear.

Integration

The issue of integration will need to be reconsidered. The nature of the argument will change. Instead of parents seeking the opportunity for their children to be educated in a comprehensive school with other children they will be looking for equal access to the same range of schools as other children.

Local education authority (LEA) policies will have less impact, and parental pressure and the admission policies of individual schools will be more influential. Integration will be much more dependent on the attitudes of school governors and headteachers.

Meeting Special Needs

Changes in secondary education may be expected to have different effects on pupils with special educational needs in two ways: whether children have Statements or not; and what kind of disability or learning difficulty gives rise to their special educational needs. Children with Statements may be more acceptable to schools because local education authorities are responsible for the additional resources required to meet their needs. Children with special needs but without a Statement, who may also require additional resources, may be less acceptable to schools. Pressure to make more children the subject of Statements may result, as may the admission of a higher percentage of children with the wider range of special needs to schools less likely to be chosen by the majority of aspiring parents.

It is evident that some disabilities and learning difficulties and the special educational needs that arise from them, are more acceptable to schools than others. For example, children with physical and sensory disabilities – such as partial sight, partial hearing and physical impairments – may be more acceptable in schools than children with learning and behaviour difficulties. As the latter form by far the largest group of all with special educational needs providing for them may prove more difficult.

The Special School

The size and staffing of special schools has always made it difficult for them to provide a broad secondary education. The requirement to deliver the National Curriculum to at least some of their pupils, whose Statements are not modified, may place impossible burdens on schools. For many the only way to provide a broad secondary curriculum will be to co-operate closely with secondary schools. This co-operation was developing well after the 1981 Education Act as research has shown (Jowett *et al.*, 1988). However, joint working arrangements are likely to be made more difficult by the financial and local management arrangements introduced by the 1988 Education Act.

Special or Regular School?

It has already been noted that where you go to school and expectations are closely related in many peoples minds. When you leave a special school do you get the same chances as a contemporary with the same needs leaving a secondary school? It is a paradox that the preparation for the next phase of transition in a secondary school may be much less adequate than that in a special school but expectations may be higher.

Starting points have been discussed as an issue because assumptions and expectations based on them must be questioned. They may limit choice and thus be handicapping.

Finishing School

Although the compulsory school stage of education ends at 16 years, what happens after that age can vary widely in this country and elsewhere. In the USA and Scandinavia 80 per cent or more of the youth age groups stay on at school up to the age of 18 + (OECD, 1990). There is no system of non-advanced further education for teenage groups but county and adult colleges offer a wide range of courses for all after the senior high school period. It is common for young people with severe disabilities to stay on in the regular senior high schools until the early twenties.

The issue in the UK is choice at 16. Although an increasing percentage of young people is staying on in full-time or part-time education either at school or in further education colleges, the overall percentage of the 16–19 age group is still not high (49 per cent in 1987; OECD, 1990).

The percentage of young people with special needs in full or part-time education after 16 is lower (Stowell, 1987).

However, unlike systems with comprehensive senior high schools the post-16 position in England and Wales is a confused and changing one. The government's introduction of a separate grant-maintained approach to further education is not likely to make individual transitions any easier for many young people including those with disabilities and learning difficulties, there are secondary schools with and without sixth forms. Where sixth forms exist, colleges of FE also provide A level work as well as a wide range of more directly vocational options. Where there are no sixth forms in secondary schools one of two alternatives may be found. There may be a sixth form college existing along side the college of FE or there may be a tertiary college. Tertiary colleges run both academic and vocational courses and thus provide all the post-16 options available in an area in one college.

The questions the 'reformed' education system needs to answer include:

- Can the system offer equal opportunities in school and FE college?
- What are the advantages and disadvantages of sixth form and tertiary colleges for students with special needs?
- Is it in the interests of their pupils for small special schools to provide post-16 education?

The same considerations, as apply to all students, should apply to those with special needs. That is to say, if the transition plan seems to suggest an aptitude for higher education or improving academic standards then staying on in school may be the best option. However, if a change of approach involving more vocationally specific education is the considered choice then the FE college could be the best option. Where neither case is strong but an atmosphere that encourages more adult attitudes and ways of learning is seen as helpful this too suggests the FE college.

It is important to recognize that many individuals with special needs may need more time to reach the same objectives. While the education system is organized on an age basis children and students with disabilities will want to work with their contemporaries. However, the end of the school stage for them should not be strictly tied to age but come at a point when achievements together with the ambience and nature of further education indicate that it is more appropriate.

Status When Finishing School

It may be important to subsequent stages of transition to recognize that at least three different administrative categories exist at the outset of transition. In the education sector the individual may be the subject of a Statement or have needs that are not thought to require a Statement.

In the social service sector the individual may be a disabled person as defined by the Disabled Persons Act (1986) and the Children Act (1989) or more correctly the National Assistance Act (1948). This last group of young people are the only ones entitled to a planned post-school programme within social service legislation.

A Statement has validity if a young person stays on in school after 16 but not if he or she attends a college of further education. Although the young person is entitled to further education, like anybody else of the same age, he or she is not entitled to the additional or different provisions of the Statement.

Similarly if an individual has special educational needs arising from a disability which require a Statement there is no guarantee that the degree of disability will fall within the 1986 Act definitions and the person thus have a legal right to a transition plan.

It must be recognized that the continuum of special needs arising from disabilities and learning difficulties is being broken up administratively as young people leave education. Social services are only responsible for young people classified as disabled in terms of the 1948 Act. Their transition plan should include contributions from all appropriate agencies. That of further and continuing education may be particularly important.

In which category the individual is placed on leaving school may have a profound effect on transition plans. There is no guarantee that most young people, whose special educational needs have been met in school, will have a transition plan, or more significantly, that anyone will be responsible for their transitional needs thereafter.

Secondary School Preparation

These considerations, important in the longer term, should not influence the programme in the final school years. Much more significant should be the objectives to be achieved and the personal qualities to be developed during that stage. Young people, including those with special educational needs, however severe, should be prepared to become independent contributing citizens who are members of a skilled and flexible workforce.

There are disagreements about the targets to be set in the different elements of the core curriculum. The balance between knowledge and skills is one of them. The National Curriculum may provide a much wider range of educational experiences for children with special educational needs in the primary and middle school years. Individuals may be more likely to start the middle years of secondary school with a common basis of experience.

Although the skills and qualities necessary for transition can developed as a result of the way the National Curriculum is delivered, the more that curriculum is modified or disapplied the more the criteria set out in this chapter should become objectives in their own right.

The CBI sets out its objectives for education in *Towards a Skills Revolution* (1989). It calls for an appropriate balance between knowledge and skills in the subjects of the National Curriculum and greater prominence for cross-curricular themes such as economic awareness and careers education. Its recommended outcomes are of interest.

In addition to the expected ones of effective communication and the applications of numeracy and technology it includes values and integrity, personal and inter-personal skills, problem solving and positive attitude to change as core elements in training and vocational education. This second group of elements is far less dependent on academic prowess. Their development is much more dependent on methodology than content.

The labour market wants to see education developing both academic proficiency and socially responsible personal skills. The attainment targets in the National Curriculum will, it is hoped, produce the first. What is less certain is whether secondary education will produce the second. Past experience suggests that the traditional attitudes and methods are not likely to.

Continuity

The role of TVEI in encouraging contact and continuity between the school and further education sector has already been mentioned. As in other phases teachers concerned with the final secondary school years should be setting their work in a continuity of curriculum and methodology. Teachers should, therefore, be well informed about their pupils' previous experience and equally well aware of the opportunities available to them in further education. Teachers and lecturers, experienced and skilled in working with young people with disabilities and learning difficulties, have much to contribute to continuity.

The objectives of the final school years should be compatible with those of the next phase of education and training. They must include the continued development of personal and life skills as well as increased attention to knowledge and skills essential to employability. Much greater collaboration between teachers and lecturers and a much greater sharing of expertise is required than is currently taking place.

Assessment for Planning and Teaching

The knowledge of what pupils know, what skills they have mastered and what gaps and difficulties exist in their knowledge and skills at any one time, are an essential prerequisite to planning a teaching programme. Equally important is an understanding of the range of individual rates and styles of learning in the group to be taught. This kind of information, gained from records and assessment, should be an integral part of teaching.

Regular assessment and the assessment of special educational needs are not different processes. The major distinction between them is a deeper knowledge of learning difficulties and the extent to which those difficulties need to be explored before planning a programme. It is a question of degree rather than a difference. This makes it all the more difficult to understand the Department of Education and Science's approach to assessment in the 1981 and 1988 Education Acts. Instead of seeing the formal assessment of special educational needs springing from the assessment of progress in the National Curriculum the two assessments are seen as apparently unrelated.

However, progress on the National Curriculum is only one element in the more comprehensive assessment which should take place to develop a transition plan for individuals with disabilities and learning difficulties. This assessment is often left until the end of the compulsory school period. The reason for carrying it out earlier is to ensure that a start can be made to acquire knowledge and skills, identified as essential to the transition plan, in the final school years.

A Transition Plan

The full scope of a transition plan will be evident after the three phases have been considered. The plan should be forward looking, covering the whole of the transition, and be in a form capable of being reviewed and modified as it is put into effect. It should start with a résumé of the individual's educational, medical, social and, where relevant, work experience. It should set out a series of goals for the individual based on opportunities in the school and neighbourhood. These goals should include the skills and knowledge to be acquired for further education and training, independent living, open or supported employment, recreation, leisure and social interaction in the community. All possible contributors to the plan should be identified as should the contributions they are to make. Detailed examples of the kind of plans being developed in the USA can be found in the publications of Sailor *et al.* (1989) and Wehman *et al.* (1988).

Inter-agency Co-operation

Although health, social services and voluntary agencies should have been working with schools from the early years it is during assessment in the latter years of secondary education that this collaboration becomes crucial if there is to be continuity of support for individuals making a transition. One of the problems is that all the major partners, education, social services and employment services, have responsibility for making a transition plan each with a separate focus, for example for further education, independent living and employment respectively.

Services are not good at contributing to a single plan and there are no obvious signs, at national or local level, of effective mechanisms for enabling them to do so. Parents, essential partners in this co-operation, often have to co-ordinate the efforts of agencies which do not naturally communicate with each other. Because the school is the starting point of transition, heads and staff should be active in involving partners in transition and, together with parents, co-ordinate their contributions to individual transition plans.

Criteria for the Secondary School Years

The criteria described in this section are equally applicable to all aspects of transition. When young people leave at sixteen, schools can only contribute to the early stages of transition. As with TVEI, the delivery of an appropriate curriculum which prepares for an adult working life necessitates very close collaboration between schools, further and continuing education and employers.

Self-Presentation

All individuals have to learn to present themselves and to argue their case in discussion. Self-advocacy is not easy for some, particularly those with severe disabilities. The delivery of the curriculum should include genuine opportunities to express preferences, to make decisions and to make a reasoned case for decisions.

Working Together

Working in groups is a skill that is vital in modern industry and society. The ability to work with others is something which can be developed when it is seen to be important. Learning can be more effective when teachers and pupils work together towards agreed objectives. Education should offer opportunities for working together in groups.

Employment

Experience and research in the USA (Hardman, 1988) and Italy (Gerry, 1989) has shown that a very high proportion of young people with severe disabilities of all kinds are able to maintain themselves in open employment in the community if they receive appropriate education and training until the twenties. The employment objective should be recognized in secondary education. Programmes should include vocational preparation reflecting local employment opportunities, training in real work situations, regular interaction with non-disabled contemporaries and experiences which enable appropriate employment to be chosen.

Independent Living

Skills necessary to live independently in the community should be developed in the school programme. They should be taught and practised in natural situations, including residential settings. The teaching programme should involve a variety of different people and places in the community.

Interaction with Non-disabled Contemporaries

Even where disabled individuals attend the same school interaction with others cannot be assumed to take place. Regular interaction between young people with and without disabilities needs to be planned and to be an integral part of a transition programme. Without such opportunities successful participation in the community may be jeopardized.

Teacher Priorities

Where the teacher has a choice of the skills and knowledge to be taught it is important to consider the objectives of transition. Particularly when working with those who are disabled priority should be given to the development of skills relevant to independent functioning within an integrated community setting.

Parental Involvement (FEU, 1989c)

Parents have a profound influence on the future of their children, particularly when they are disabled. Parental involvement in transition programmes is essential. They have many concerns about their children and need to be able to discuss their secondary education and the implications of developing self-advocacy, independence and participation in the community.

Discussions with families and young people about future opportunities need to begin well before leaving school and must be sustained. Where parents are unable, for any reason, to take a constructive part in planning their childrens' future, schools should identify another advocate, acceptable to the young person, to guide them through the maze of transition possibilities.

Orientation

Effective teaching for transition should encourage student choice and individual preferences. Programmes should include a commitment to personal support during transition, experiences of integration in the local environment, real work in integrated settings and the effective use of community resources. The task will be to adhere to these principles within the framework of the National Curriculum. It will be easier with young people with severe disabilities and learning difficulties where their Statements may modify the requirements of that framework.

A start should be made to provide a relevant education from the end of the second secondary year and records should be kept to enable those responsible in the post-school period to provide continuity. Where a young person stays on in school over the age of 16, and is not following traditional examination courses, this orientation towards living and working competences should be paramount.

CHAPTER 5

Further and Continuing Education

The three main elements in this sector – further education, the youth service and adult and continuing education – are often seen as separate and independent services. In the past they have tended to work in isolation from each other. However, there is increasing evidence that links are being built between them. All of them may provide continuing support during transition.

In the past, further education in colleges for young people aged between 16 and 19 years was quite distinct from education in schools. In recent years the development of tertiary colleges, where all those aged between 16 and 19 can follow courses of study previously available in sixth forms and further education colleges, has begun to overcome this separation.

While each element in further and continuing education has a specific role, all may well be providing learning opportunities for the same individuals at different stages of their lives. They need to become partners in offering a comprehensive service, through adolescence to adulthood.

The government's proposal for a separate, centrally funded further education sector, with grant-maintained status for colleges, may help to develop a more coherent pattern of provision which is relevant both to young people and to employers. However, sixth forms in schools will continue to compete for smaller age groups and limited resources and provision for minority needs may be at risk.

The Background

Until twenty years ago, further education, in association with employer apprenticeship schemes and professional training requirements, could be seen as providing most of the vocational preparation available to young people. It was essentially a selective system providing full-time, part-time, day and block release for courses designed to meet the requirements of a given range of occupations.

The content of these courses was based on what professionals, colleges and employers, together with examining bodies, thought should be the skills and knowledge necessary for a given level of operation in industry and commerce. This time-limited, course-based structure served colleges well, and employers perhaps less well but gave little attention to individual student needs. Individuals took what was on offer, fitting in to the available pattern and sometimes found themselves on inappropriate courses. This traditional approach failed to respond to the continuing educational needs of many low-achieving school leavers.

Some years ago the government of the time became increasingly concerned about high levels of youth unemployment, particularly among low achievers, and about their inadequate preparation for work. Considerable funds were redirected, through a separate agency, to vocational preparation in a variety of youth training schemes. The clear objective of this agency was vocational preparation. It was expected to buy in the most appropriate form of preparation for different client groups.

The agency, first called Manpower Services, more latterly the Training Agency (TA) and now the Training, Education and Enterprise Directorate (TEED) has had many changes of name and function. Its original concerns covered all training and retraining with a particular emphasis on young people leaving school and those who were unemployed. With the setting up of Training and Enterprise Councils (TECs) its role is significantly diminished.

There was some mutual antagonism between the agency and further education in the early days. The agency's approach was characterized by a marked concentration on vocational preparation to the exclusion of other educational dimensions. Further education was seen as more concerned with a broadly based education for specific vocational areas. It was not considered to be meeting the needs of the whole ability range in the community or providing adequate preparation for work in all levels of industry and commerce.

The shock delivered by the setting up of a rival agency for vocational preparation resulted in further education reconsidering its role. The agency was selective in its approach to the courses it financed, requiring a structure with clear objectives, an instrumental approach to learning and performance criteria for evaluation. Colleges were confronted with the need to provide for a wider client group particularly when delivering courses for the agency. It was against this background that further education began to respond to the needs of those with disabilities and learning difficulties.

Recent Educational Legislation

The Education Reform Act 1988 (ERA) did not have such a dramatic impact on further education as it had on the compulsory school period. Proposed legislation may have a more radical effect. Further education has been accustomed to a fair degree of autonomy in such matters as budgeting and course development. The Act has increased this autonomy by giving governing bodies and institutions more powers and changing the role of the local authority.

Individual institutions have been making provision for students with special needs for some years, but the 1988 Act was the first time that the needs of people with disabilities and learning difficulties had been mentioned in further education legislation. Although the requirement is couched in very general terms, implementing the Act must include meeting the needs of these students (FEU, 1988b).

The Act requires the LEA to produce a three year strategic plan (FEU, 1989a) for all further education. This plan is similar to that required by the TEED for 'work related non-advanced further education'. It must include arrangements to meet the needs of *all* students and thus provides a basis for the development of provision to meet special needs. Colleges are required to produce a development plan to implement their part of the LEA's strategic plan. While LEAs may retain some funds for central services and excepted items, the Act requires that almost all available finance is handled by colleges. Formula funding determines college budgets. The LEA, in consultation with colleges, gives a weighting to each area of college activity.

It is too soon after the implementation of the Act to know how this process is working and whether it is an effective means of funding students with disabilities and learning difficulties. However, some issues are already emerging. Few LEAs or colleges have devised a system for analysing and determining the level of additional funding required to support students with disabilities or learning difficulties. Most are relying on previous budget allocations, often based on separate class or course groups. Few are yet basing requirements on the assessment of individual student needs especially where students are being supported in an integrated setting. There is a danger that funding will encourage provision in discrete groups.

Another requirement of the 1988 Act is for LEAs to make clear the criteria they propose to use to monitor and evaluate the quality of the work of colleges. This evaluation is to be based on agreed performance indicators to enable comparisons to be made between institutions. The information gained from evaluation is to be fed back into the LEA planning cycle to improve effectiveness and efficiency. The process of evaluation and the criteria chosen should cover provision for *all* students. Criteria must also take into account how provision is resourced. Although it is not clear how performance indicators will be chosen, it will not be surprising if the choice is influenced by methods used to monitor the delivery of the National Curriculum in schools. The ways in which performance criteria are conceived, chosen and interpreted will have a significant impact on provision for students with disabilities and learning difficulties.

However, taking these students' needs into account should not lessen the rigour of the performance criteria selected nor the rigour with which they are applied. Those with disabilities and learning difficulties are not well served by low standards, sloppy programmes and ill-defined performance criteria.

Whilst some authorities are using their former advisers as an inspection team to monitor quality, effectiveness and efficiency, other authorities are looking at external systems such as industrial quality assurance strategies to evaluate performance. Two examples are the BSI Industrial Standards (BSI 57/50) and Japanese Total Quality Management schemes (TEED, 1990). One of the dangers of such schemes is that outcomes may be overemphasized and less attention may be paid to the process of education.

An overemphasis on the product could result in colleges having less control over the curriculum with the result that their programmes become dominated by employment competence criteria. It is worth noting that employers and the CBI report (CBI, 1989) emphasize the importance of personal skills to successful employment. A proper balance between process and product needs to be struck.

Other Recent Legislation

Legislation influencing transition has been discussed in Chapter 3. Two recent Acts – the Children Act (1989) and The National Health Service and Community Care Act (1990) – have particular relevance for further and continuing education. Care in the community involves transitions for which preparation is necessary (FEU, 1988a).

This legislation is likely to have an impact on post-school educational facilities in two ways:

1. The education and support of people, who are the concern of health and social services, during transition.
2. The training of professional staff in all agencies for changed patterns of work.

Curriculum Continuity and Progression with Schools

Until recently, further and continuing education has been based on a pattern of discrete courses each with its own curriculum. Except when providing GCSE and A level courses there has been little curriculum continuity with schools. However, one or two initiatives in recent years have drawn attention to the need for continuity between school and college and provided some useful examples of working partnerships.

One of them, the TVEI which began in September 1983, has been influential in forming such links. It was conceived as a four year programme to encourage the development of a vocational element into the last two compulsory school years which could subsequently be built on by FE colleges. Although school/college link courses have existed for some time, it is one of the few planned links between school and college. To qualify for funding LEAs have to submit schemes showing how vocational preparation will be enhanced within the school curriculum and how the scheme will be implemented and evaluated.

The initiative was intended for pupils of all levels of ability but in practice, although available to all, it has been introduced most widely with less academic pupils. Most special schools only became involved in the scheme after it had been running for a few years.

Where TVEI has been successful it has led to the planning of a four year programme spanning school and college. A more appropriate curriculum for many young people has evolved including opportunities to experience a number of vocational options. It has provided continuity and progression as individuals move from school to further education. Improved resources have been made available to schools and partnership between the staff of schools, special schools and colleges, including joint staff development, has been fostered.

Related initiatives such as the Compact Scheme, which started in the London area, have also linked secondary schools to industries and courses in further education. A similar scheme in Leicester, where all 14–16 year olds enter the scheme as equal partners, includes special schools (SKILL, 1990). Industrial and commercial enterprises are linked with individual schools to support school programmes, provide work experience and youth training scheme places and guarantee a number of jobs for pupils from the school who reach agreed standards.

The introduction of the National Curriculum has diverted attention and effort from TVEI and it is now to be wound up. However, the National Curriculum should ensure that all those entering further education will have their achievements recorded in a standard form providing better evidence of attainments than has usually been available in the past.

Accreditation

The accreditation of further education courses was, until recently, undertaken by a variety of agencies. It was based on prescribed courses of study over a specified time. These agencies will continue to administer schemes of accreditation but within a national framework. The setting up of the National Vocational Qualifications Scheme (FEU, 1990a; NROVA, 1990) is an attempt to develop a single system of accreditation in which different levels of competence are agreed with the industries and services for which they are designed. Progress through a system of National Vocational Qualifications (NVQs) will be recorded on a National Record of Vocational Achievement (NROVA) commonly referred to as the National Record.

The NVQ scheme changes the emphasis from courses to learner-led and negotiated individual programmes which recognize and build on prior learning. Outcomes, with a new emphasis on competence as well as knowledge, are assessed when the individual can demonstrate appropriate skills and knowledge and not at the end of fixed periods. Students may well arrive at colleges able to demonstrate some competences learned elsewhere.

It would seem sensible to build an individual's National Record on the basis of his or her National Curriculum Record of Achievement. Some discussions are taking place which may lead to closer links. Similarly, a small working group (including representatives of the FEU, NVQ Council, Secondary Education Accreditation Council (SEAC) and TEED) is considering 'core skills' (FEU, 1990b). The group is hoping to produce proposals, in the form of a consultation document, for 'core units' to be integrated into both vocational and academic courses. For students following NVQ programmes these units would be built in to levels 1–4 of the scheme. If such an initiative is supported it would ensure that all students were given the opportunity to acquire a common core of competences and would provide a common basis for assessing progress during transition.

If NVQs are to become requirements for employment it is crucial that all students have access to them. Throughout the development of NVQ attention has been paid to this feature but colleges may have to examine and redesign their organizational structures if they are to meet a wider range of individual needs and to encourage increased participation.

Learner-led individual programmes, with a more flexible time scale, will also require that assessment, guidance and counselling is available to students to help them develop appropriate individual programmes. This approach should provide new and wider opportunities for students with disabilities and learning difficulties.

Training and Enterprise Councils

The setting up of the Manpower Services Agency and its subsequent transformations has already been mentioned. The latest step in moving responsibility for vocational preparation and training to employers is the setting up of Training and Enterprise Councils to cover all regions of the country. The idea behind these Councils is that they will work with other agencies in their areas, including LEAs and colleges, to produce a coherent pattern of training responsive to local needs. Councils will not only be concerned with training during transition from school but also with retraining and updating skills as local labour market requirements change. The new arrangements have involved a major transfer of funds from TEED to these Councils. A number of recent publications set out their aims (Business and Community, 1990).

It will be essential to ensure, through appropriate representation, that Councils address the needs of all people living in their areas and that, within an equal opportunity policy, they make adequate provision for those with special needs. Councils should be required to produce a balance sheet in which successful training and employment is weighed against unemployment. This is vital to ensure that disadvantaged groups and those with limited achievements on leaving school are being offered appropriate opportunities.

Training Credits

The setting up of TECs has been accompanied by the introduction of training credits (DE, 1990). These involve the allocation of vouchers which individuals can use to gain the training of their choice. Training may be provided in colleges of further education, by employers or by independent training agencies.

There are a number of uncertainties about the proposals which experience may resolve. For example, will individuals have responsibilities for their own choice of programme, and, in voucher experiments, for the finance involved? It is not yet clear whether training credits will actually go to individuals or be channelled through professionals or employers. If the responsibility is placed on individuals it will be necessary to provide counselling and advice about the best use of their opportunities. This will be particularly important for some individuals with special needs.

A major concern is the value of training credits. If they are of equal value this may affect the choice of programme and possibly the choice of the cheapest option rather than the most appropriate. If the value of vouchers is to be varied according to the level of training this too may work against the interests of those who are disadvantaged. If those with disabilities are to receive vouchers to a higher value will this be based on premature decisions about employability? It is too early to say what the contribution of training credits will be to the transition of those with special needs. They could provide students with an extended or enhanced period of training.

Partnership

It must be emphasized that arrangements for effective transition involve a partnership between many agencies. Further and continuing education cannot be the sole supporter of individuals. Colleges are not in a position to be responsible for individual transitions nor are they necessarily an obvious co-ordinating agency.

Present practice suggests that lecturers and tutors in the field have recognized that proper planning and support must be provided in partnership with others but this is difficult to implement in the absence of established frameworks and a lack of recognition by management of the importance of such frameworks.

Working with partners is not a new phenomenon in further education where structures for working with industry and employers have existed for a long time but inter-agency working is a more complex process. Although individual members of staff have developed their own networks to support students, these personal networks are often dependent on individuals in fields where there is considerable movement and change and thus they are sometimes transient and not securely set in an organizational framework.

A major implication of the new legislation is its endorsement of inter-agency planning and shared responsibility for the implementation of individual programmes. However, financing remains fragmented and related to each agency's budget and this restricts what is possible. Even where joint financing of projects is possible different planning cycles and different agency priorities make combined operations hard to put into effect.

The range of agencies to which an individual may need access and with which colleges need to remain in contact is wide. Each agency also should be aware of the work of others. The network of college links that may need to be established is illustrated in Figure 2.

Looking Ahead

There are considerable changes taking place in further and continuing education. Its importance is being increasingly recognized and its contribution to effective vocational preparation stressed. The views of employers, via the CBI, and the employees, via the Trades Union Council (TUC), agree with those of many managers of further education.

Figure 2

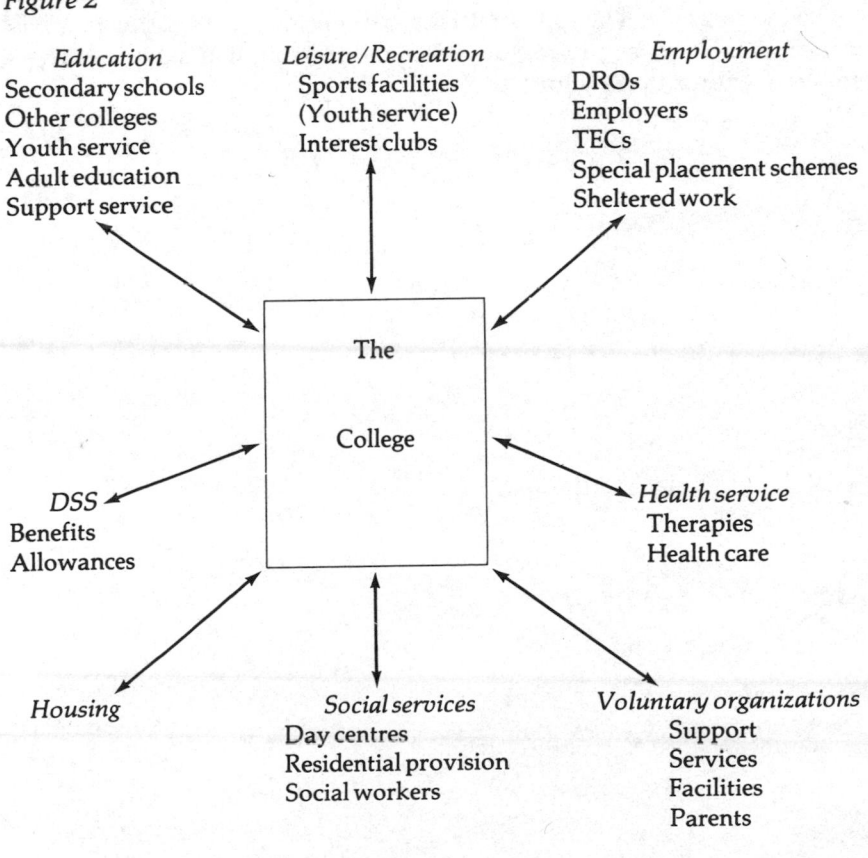

What is required is a flexible system of training (FEU, 1988c) in which a 'core' of social and general employment skills and competences are developed (FEU, 1989d). Increased individual choice should be backed up by resources based on the establishment of appropriate weightings which themselves should be reflected in the value of training credits. All these developments have the potential to increase opportunities for disadvantaged groups.

Further and continuing education will become more autonomous with a more business-like approach to management. More emphasis will be placed on the outcomes and competences to be expected on the completion of individual programmes. But, there are important continuities which should not be lost in these changes such as the development of personal and social skills and responsible citizenship. These are not necessarily the outcomes of a narrowly focused vocational education.

Far too few young people are well prepared for employment and adult life. Smaller age groups require that everyone, including those with disabilities, have access to higher and further education and to good vocational preparation. The role of further and continuing education is crucial in providing both access to education and training and subsequently to employment for those young people.

CHAPTER 6

Colleges

Education for young people in the 16–19 age range takes place in four settings: sixth forms, sixth form colleges, tertiary colleges and FE colleges. FE colleges exist alongside secondary school sixth forms and sixth form colleges and compete for the same, 16–19, age group. Tertiary colleges provide for *all* post-16 students in an area and also serve as bases for non-vocational adult education. One significant difference between the sixth form and the tertiary college is that they are subject to different regulations. The former are subject to Schools Regulations and the latter to Further Education Regulations. The government's proposed changes will bring sixth form colleges under the same regulations as further education colleges but different regulations will still govern sixth forms in secondary schools. The proposed changes are unlikely to facilitate the coherent planning of post-16 opportunities.

The work of tertiary colleges ranges from traditional sixth-form work through the whole spectrum of pre-vocational and vocational opportunities. In the discussion of further education that follows it should be assumed that it concerns the work both of FE and of tertiary colleges.

The Nature of Further Education

Further education has always been a service whose existence has been dependent on responding to the needs of industry and commerce by providing appropriate courses of study. Subject to different legislation from the school sector its inclusion in the Education Act 1988 gave it more control over staffing and budgeting.

Colleges have delivered further and continuing education with increasing flexibility, for example full-time and part-time courses, block-release and day-release courses and twilight and night courses. More recently outreach programmes in industry and commerce have become common. Expansion has also involved a greater contribution in the community; for example, in day and residential centres of all kinds. Many colleges have also extended the period of time in a year over which they provide courses.

Forward planning is vital but must make allowances for last-minute adjustments as colleges respond to their local market. Reasons for last-minute adjustments include:

- The late receipt of examination results by school leavers.
- Young people's varying employment prospects between leaving school and enrolling in further education.
- Competitive local recruitment.

For some students the college is a natural progression from school, while for others it provides a second chance. Some young people consider college a more adult alternative to the sixth form. Other school leavers may be attracted by the practical nature of many options, some of which provide an alternative route to higher education. Colleges also provide important opportunities for:

- Adult learning later in life.
- Retraining following changes in employment practices or redundancy.
- Members of disadvantaged groups, without previous access, to be introduced to further education.

The funding and facilities of colleges have been based on the need to offer students the best examples of industrial, commercial and service industrial practices. These vary according to local and regional patterns of employment. Thus colleges may be expected to have an appropriate range of workshops, studios, laboratories and technology suites which are adapted for teaching purposes but which also reflect the best employment standards.

Access to Colleges

In 1990 there were 458 further and higher education institutions in England. They are distributed haphazardly, clustering in conurbations and often far apart in rural areas. Present provision results in marked inequalities of opportunity over the country as a whole. Although transport arrangements are made, and residential accommodation provided in some instances, the range of choice available to students is not the same in all areas. Students with disabilities and learning difficulties, in urban areas, generally find it easier to make appropriate arrangements.

When provision for students with disabilities and learning difficulties was first introduced it was often low status and accommodated in annexes sometimes apart from the main college. However, attitudes have changed, work of quality has raised the status of provision and there has been steady progress in adapting college buildings and providing purpose-built facilities. It is now common for physical access to all aspects of further and continuing education to receive serious attention.

Access to Courses

Most colleges are responding to the needs of a far wider range of students than was the case 15 years ago. A report commissioned by the DES, *Catching Up* published in 1987 (Stowell, 1987) shows the position at that time. As it was the first research of its kind the extent of this response is hard to quantify. Subsequent plans to review progress five years later, originally announced publicly by a Departmental Minister, have not been carried out. Such a review would be of value to planners as the percentage growth in this expanding area of provision could be determined.

Many decisions are undoubtedly being taken without an adequate data base at both national and local levels, although local education authorities and colleges are trying to improve their information gathering systems.

Colleges must be aware of all the 'markets' they should serve. These include a significant percentage of individuals with limited school achievements, not served very well until the Training Agency provided money, and adolescents and adults with a wide array of disabilities and learning difficulties. Demographic trends have also led to changes in the composition and age structure of the student population. There has been a steady increase in courses designed to attract older students. Students with disabilities have not been recruited to these initiatives to the extent that might be expected. This probably reflects their limited employment opportunities. All too often they are not considered an integral part of the potential workforce by the agencies responsible for meeting their needs.

College Management

Governors are now responsible for the management of colleges. The official recommendation that one governor should have a particular interest in special needs is a beginning. But a single individual is unlikely to have much influence unless the governing body as a whole is sensitive to all the educational needs that the college might serve.

A prerequisite to modern administration is a 'mission statement' to set out the college's philosophy and intentions. It is in this statement that one would expect to see the college's approach to equal opportunities (FEU, 1990c) in relation to race, gender and disability. If colleges produce a positive mission statement it may help to create the favourable conditions for this important aspect of their work and enable them to evaluate the extent to which intentions are realized in practice.

Colleges are also required to have a development plan outlining how they intend to respond to the authority's strategic plan and the changing demands of further education. Individual programmes and the performance criteria by which the college will evaluate its own work will be two important elements in college plans.

The traditional pattern of college management has evolved from a departmental structure. In this structure a senior management team is supported by heads of departments usually responsible for predominently vocationally grouped courses. Each area of work within a department is managed by a course co-ordinator responsible for a course team which in turn is responsible for groups of students enrolled on particular courses.

This structure, when applied to meeting special needs, tends to lead to the establishment of separate courses and sometimes makes it difficult for staff to support individual students with disabilities following other courses elsewhere in colleges.

New demands made on colleges, including the delivery of individually negotiated learning programmes in a more flexible manner, make the traditional management structure no longer appropriate. As a result many colleges are undergoing radical reorganizations. One result has been a move away from a rigid course structure to teams or faculties responsible for areas of the curriculum. There is an increased emphasis on information gathering, improved communication, increased participation rates and expansion. Other developments have included extending general learning resources, such as libraries, study facilities and basic skills workshops, and making them more accessible to all students and more appropriate for students with special needs.

A focus within the college, such as an equal opportunities forum, for studying and meeting the needs of students with disabilities and learning difficulties is essential. The promotion of equal opportunities should be the responsibility of a senior manager if provision for students with special needs is to be an integral part of the college programme. It will be a disadvantage if the forum is a permanent committee which might be seen to absolve the college as a whole from concern for special needs.

It may be better to set up a small time-limited task force to evaluate current arrangements for these students and to provide a programme for the development of access to all college facilities and of appropriate support services. The tasks and responsibilities to be undertaken by college management, stimulated by the task force, involves attention to such areas as resource allocation, disability awareness programmes, liaison with other agencies, curriculum development, student counselling and learning support services. These responsibilities should also include monitoring and evaluating the effectiveness of the facilities and services provided.

The establishment of criteria and standards for special needs work, backed up with appropriate resources, is crucial. Separate courses and facilities may have a place but they should not characterize provision. Most will serve a bridging function. All sectors of the institution should contribute to meeting special needs. Staff working with students with disabilities and learning difficulties should be able to provide the necessary support to both other staff and students in order to meet learning needs anywhere in the college.

Students with Disabilities and Learning Difficulties

It was the Warnock Report that drew attention to the need for the development of further education opportunities. Although, prior to that, limited provision had been made for some students with physical and sensory disabilities, the development of further education was one of the Report's three priority areas.

Whilst the government of the time showed little enthusiasm for post-school provision its recommendations were nevertheless taken up by individual colleges. Parents exerted pressure in various ways. The careers service also lobbied colleges to provide something for students with special needs as there were few other opportunities for them.

Apart from some small schemes for students with physical and sensory disabilities, college initiatives mainly provided for young people with moderate learning difficulties who could not find employment. Some courses were set up. Many, without clear aims, made use of uncommitted staff time and any available college accommodation, however inappropriate. The curriculum was undeveloped and often undemanding. Many staff were redeployed to run the courses. Where special staff were recruited they usually came from special schools, with little understanding of further education. In some instances they recreated school environments and programmes in colleges. This did little for students and even less for the status of the work in colleges. It was not surprising that if colleges could keep their numbers up with more prestigious students they usually tried to do so.

However, there were a number of important innovators in individual colleges who developed provision to the point where a uniquely further education approach to meeting special needs is now evident. They received support from a number of sources. SKILL, the National Bureau for Students with Disabilities, has campaigned very effectively on behalf of students with disabilities.

The Further Education Unit, whose remit is the support of curriculum development, has made a significant contribution by undertaking a number of projects to identify the needs of disabled students and suggesting suitable approaches to the curriculum to meet their needs (FEU/NFER, 1982). The Unit has also made it clear that many of the main elements in successful provision for these students are equally relevant to *all* students in further education. For example, much can be learned from studying effective educational arrangements for students with special needs, by other staff seeking to implement individual learning programmes.

Colleges now expect to include provision for a variety of special needs within their policies and programmes. They are becoming practiced in working with other agencies, particularly in employment training, and are ready to take on board individual special needs in collaboration with social services, TECs and other agencies.

The range of students who may require support is now wide. It ranges from those who may require occasional support on account of intermittent learning problems, or more sustained support due to specific difficulties, to students with profound and complex intellectual disabilities and learning difficulties. They may be found anywhere in a college and not just in discrete groups.

The majority of students come straight from schools but the number of adults is also increasing. There is another small, but significant, group of post-traumatic disabled students often requiring a very specialized and individual response. These may include individuals who have deteriorating disabilities, post-stroke complications and other conditions. The accidents that may occur in the risk taking of young people may also result in disabilities. All of these students may find it necessary to reappraise their ambitions and life plans and profit from further education in reshaping them.

Provision to Meet Special Needs

In the past there have been three main types of provision for these students in colleges: supporting arrangements for students on regular courses, bridging courses and separate courses. While the objectives of the first two forms of provision are the same for all students, separate courses have often been very unclear in their aims. These courses are sometimes seen by parents as delaying entry to day training centres rather than positive preparation for the next stage of independence.

It is important to recognize that the majority of further education colleges have to respond to a wide range of learning needs and few can expect to concentrate only on those associated with a particular disability. This response requires a complex network of support both within the institution and outside it.

The provision made within the college will usually be the responsibility of the Co-ordinator or Head of the Support Team. The person concerned is likely to be involved in a number of overlapping networks:

- A management network – the governing board, the college senior management group and heads of faculties.
- A college services network – the marketing and publicity section, counselling and guidance staff, medical and nursing staff, welfare staff and students union staff.
- A related educational network – all staff across all disciplines who may be involved in work with students with particular disabilities in college or in outreach work.

The external networks will be even more complicated since they may involve all the contributors to transition listed in Chapter 2. However, it is possible to identify some of the most important links: LEA officers and advisers, TEC and TA, health services, psychology services, careers service, youth service, adult education, social services, employers and various specialists in specific disabilities.

It may be helpful to provide a check-list of the facilities and services a college might be expected to provide in addition to good management. Elements with relevance to meeting special needs should be recognized in the following areas:

1. Organization:
   - an equal opportunities policy statement;
   - a three-year development plan (with special needs included);
   - a flexible range of provision for all students which is designed to respond to a wide range of individual variations in style and pace of learning;
   - a fair and equitable distribution of resources and staff to all aspects of college work including support for students with special needs;
   - weightings for programmes and support for individuals which acknowledge varying levels of need;
   - a clear system of liaison with schools and other agencies, including employers, for the entry of students to the college, their continued support and their entry into work;
   - admission procedures, with information in appropriate forms, which

facilitate the application for places by potential students with disabilities and learning difficulties;
- a student counselling and guidance system which is sensitive to the issues that arise when students have special needs;
- the use of clear performance indicators, similar in rigour to those used throughout the college, to evaluate the quality of the education offered to students with special needs.

2. Management:
   - a governing board member with knowledge of meeting special needs in further education;
   - a member of the senior management group with direct responsibility for special needs provision;
   - a college co-ordinator with responsibility for developing and sustaining a high level of learning support for students with all kinds of special needs, for liaison with all college staff and for leading a learning support team;
   - a staff team responsible for meeting special needs in collaboration with colleagues in the college and with specialist supporting agencies outside the college.

3. Marketing and finance:
   - staff responsible for marketing the college with a brief to include students with special needs in their range of activities;
   - finance staff aware of the means of funding students with special needs, familiar with all statutory and voluntary sources of support for them.

4. Buildings and accommodation:
   - disabled access to the site and to all buildings with a plan, where necessary, for improving access;
   - a survey of all the college facilities and their availability to and appropriateness for disabled students together with a plan to improve their use;
   - suitable parking and toilet facilities for disabled students;
   - libraries and other resource areas with materials and equipment to make them accessible to disabled students;
   - a suitable learning support centre and where necessary specialist accommodation.

5. The curriculum:
   - admission procedures which include appropriate assessment arrangements to determine curriculum starting points for students with special needs;
   - students with special needs recognized as having the same curriculum entitlements as other students (FEU, 1989e);
   - a clear structure of learning opportunities, with maximum access to

the same curricula as others, which provide continuity and progression for the individual;
- a range of appropriate equipment and materials to support individual learning throughout the college;
- individual programmes primarily negotiated with the student but discussed with all concerned.

6. Support systems:
- access to college counselling and guidance services;
- tutorial support for all students with time allocations specific to the nature and complexity of individual need;
- health service and psychological service support available;
- welfare personnel for the support of individual students;
- links with external statutory and voluntary support services.

This check-list is not a blueprint. Many other items could be listed. What it does attempt to do is to show meeting special needs as an integral part of a college's response to its local community and not simply something added on which is discrete and different from other provision.

The Management of Transition

If the process of transition is to be properly managed some attention must be given to a framework for planning and providing facilities and services. A framework is necessary for the transition of all students from school to an adult working life and the same framework should meet the needs of students with disabilities and learning difficulties. However, from time to time there may be a need for some additional groups for planning and evaluation within an LEA area. These might include:

- A forum for local authority policy development.
- An officers group (further education, social services, health, employment and social security) to look at cross-service issues.
- A specialist group concerned with meeting the needs of children and young people with disabilities and learning difficulties from the early years to adulthood.
- A group within each institution or service.

There are certain tasks common to all of them, such as ensuring that all policies and practices include attention to special needs, to setting up special arrangements where necessary and monitoring their effectiveness as well as ensuring that managing transition is fitted into a framework of services for all students.

The existence of different groups does not ensure appropriate provision unless there is effective communication between them. Figure 3 illustrates one suggested pattern of communication.

There is a need for specialist groups both to ensure that particular special needs are not overlooked but also to look at the continuity of provision and services between pre-school, school and post-school. Such groups should be seen as task forces with a limited life rather than as permanent elements. It is difficult to be precise about membership but the group should provide a focus for special needs concerns with a particular emphasis on the continuity necessary during transition from one phase to another. Members might include administrators from the school and post-school sector, heads of schools, colleges and adult education services, parents, students, representatives of other agencies and facilities.

General planning and management groups need information and realistic plans for meeting special needs and this may be a job for such a task force of limited life which might also consider the development and implementation of individual transition plans. The ultimate aim of all work with those with special needs should be to meet their needs within the normal range of facilities and services for all.

Figure 3

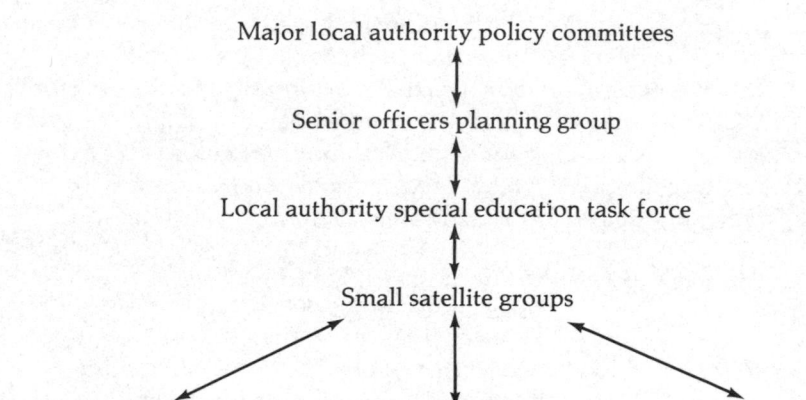

Criteria

At both the beginning and end of further education the overall objectives of transition should be reviewed. The focus should be the management of transition during the college period. These questions need to be asked:

- How are colleges involved in transition planning teams?
- What information (including standard assessments in school) is available prior to an individual attending college?
- What guidance and counselling facilities are available?
- How are students assessed on entry?
- How are individual programmes, including 'core skills', negotiated, managed and reviewed?
- Is this an active process designed to involve and benefit the individual?

All too often the college adopts a passive role in which the management of individual transitions has a low priority.

Other criteria should include transition outcomes such as employment, autonomy, social interaction, adult family roles and the quality of the total experience.

Employment

This should be a major objective of further education for all students. Building on individual strengths and appropriate experiences, colleges should be preparing for vocational and life choices. One of the strengths of further education is the range of vocational opportunities it can offer and which a student can sample. Within the curriculum there should be clear evidence of vocational preparation, work experience, active support for access to employment and close links with other agencies to ensure continuing support in employment where necessary.

Personal Autonomy, Independence and Adult Status

Some young people with special needs enter colleges without having very much control over their lives. It is important that further education provides the opportunities to broaden relationships, experiment with a range of activities, handle personal spending and explore independence and inter-dependence in a managed environment. Curriculum design should recognize the need for opportunities to develop these skills. The FE college offers an adult environment but the degree to which an individual will achieve these goals will vary as will their rate of progress towards them.

At the end of their further education students with disabilities and learning difficulties should be able to achieve a degree of autonomy, independence and adult status. They should be able to find their way about their environment, express preferences, choose activities and manage their time and money. Only if these skills are developed will the individual be enabled to make a successful transition to employment.

Social Interaction, Community Participation, Leisure and Recreation

These aspects of personal development are not just 'out of college' activities. They are important elements to recognize and include in all programmes preparing students for employment and leisure.

Achieving these criteria is not solely the responsibility of colleges. Other agencies such as the youth service, adult and continuing education have important contributions to make. All concerned should aim to help students establish links with other providers in the neighbourhood.

Criteria in this area by which to judge competences might include the young person knowing the opportunities available in the area, having a chosen activity in which proficiency is being achieved, being able to function in the local community and make appropriate responses in common social situations.

Adult Family Roles

Families and friends, as well as other agencies, make an important contribution to the development of an individual's relationships and family roles. The college curriculum often provides a last opportunity for informed discussion and guidance about this area of personal development. It is not sufficient to deal with young people and effective parents. Where students may be disadvantaged by the lack of support they receive from their families, links should be made with other agencies to provide it in the final stages of transition.

Does the individual have personal space and time within the family? Are more adult relationships recognized and being developed? Is independent living accepted and prepared for? These are some of the questions which outline the criteria in this area of transition, and emphasize the need for all participants to be involved in a transition plan.

Conclusion

Further education is entering a new phase in which the intention is to recognize the individual learner, rather than the course, as the main focus for college activities. A core curriculum is being discussed as is the concept of 'curriculum entitlement'. Programmes of life-long learning for individuals will be based on previous learning and assessed competences.

Such an approach has long been best practice in work with students with special needs. They are encouraged to use their own preferred way of working towards agreed goals. Staff have developed a high level of skill in analysing learning difficulties and planning the most appropriate learning and teaching strategies to overcome them (FEU, 1990d).

Further education now needs these skills applied to all students. There is a unique opportunity for special needs staff to make a wider contribution in colleges through work with colleagues and other students. If this opportunity is not taken there is a real danger that work with students with special needs will become increasingly isolated from the main stream of further education and separate provision, without full access to college facilities, become more common.

When looking at the nature of provision within further education five major aspects are important. Ideas, aspirations and positive attitudes to all students are a vital prerequisite. The authority's strategic plan must be clear about how special needs are to be met. Governors and senior managers must develop a clear policy framework for colleges. This requires a hard look at available resources and clear decisions about local priorities. There needs to be a statement of the facilities and services it is possible to provide from which to develop individual programmes which are part of a transition plan.

Ideas, aspirations and attitudes are what this book is about. It will be important that all those concerned – from the governing board to junior staff and students – are involved in a healthy dialogue about ideas and aspirations. This should inform the college policy and help to determine priorities.

Changes in further education offer an ideal opportunity for support teaching for special needs to become an integral, albeit specialized, part of what is offered to all learners. The effective transition of young people with special needs requires that their programmes are a natural variant of what is available to their contemporaries. How these programmes are to be negotiated, offering more open access to the curriculum together with appropriate support, should be high on the college agenda.

In each phase of transition individuals are expected to make many adjustments. A major question is whether institutions, such as colleges, are able to adapt by accommodating a wider range of learners. One important step in the process is to carry out an educational audit (FEU, 1989f) to see whether the college's aims are appropriate to the neighbourhood and the customers they are expected to serve including those with special needs.

CHAPTER 7

Employment and Independent Living

The outcomes of parenting, education and training become clear during the third stage of transition. Questions about the outcomes for children and young people with severe, profound and complex disabilities must be asked. Is their education expected to lead anywhere? Have they just been given a semblance of normality without any objective? When there is stress on accountability, it is also pertinent to ask what return is expected on investment in 10–15 years of education? Should it lead to any saving of care costs or contribution through employment, and if so does it?

The *ad hoc* nature of thinking about outcomes is illustrated by the lack of clear goals for transition, the slow development of post-school education and training opportunities and above all by the paucity of opportunities for a positive and contributing life in the community afterwards. 'Care in the Community', in some ways a very positive concept, is a rather patronizing approach perhaps appropriate for the declining years but no prescription for the life of a young disabled individual. Adult status involves working and the capacity to live independently but these aspects of life are often dealt with quite separately by different agencies.

Adult Status

There are, of course, a number of aspects of adulthood. The most obvious is the legal status accorded at eighteen but before that there are other legal milestones. Although work and independent living are essential elements in status as an adult, probably the most potent indicators are the attitudes and behaviours of parents, professionals and contemporaries. It is the recognition of a personal and psychological adulthood which may be most important to the individual.

The four main areas in which adulthood is achieved have already been noted:

- personal autonomy and responsibility for one's own life;
- productive activity, useful work and economic self-sufficiency;
- social interaction and community participation;
- roles within the family as a non-dependent young adult, spouse or parent.

Have the previous stages of transition enabled the individual to reach these objectives in the third stage? Have voluntary and statutory agencies and professionals recognized the right of a disabled young person to an adult status or is 'eternal childhood' the implicit model for post-school provision and services?

Work

Most disabled young people see work as vital to their life. It gives them status, independence and choice. Failure to obtain paid employment increases their handicaps. *Enabled to Work*, which is part of the FEU *Working Together*? package gives the views of young people and employers (FEU, 1989c).

However, work has not always been an expectation or an objective. The day activity centre with engagement in relatively trivial time passing activity was, and is, seen as wholly appropriate for some. As late as 1978 the Warnock Report was developing the idea of 'significant living without work'. There is still some doubt whether entry into employment for young people with severe disabilities and learning difficulties is now being taken seriously. The range of employment opportunities, including self-employment and working from home, is being increased by information technology. Smaller youth groups entering the labour market make it essential for economies to support the preparation for employment of disadvantaged groups including those with disabilities and learning difficulties. Work should be the expectation.

Sheltered work has always been available for adults wounded in wars and disabled in industry but has not always been available to young people with disabilities and learning difficulties leaving school. OECD set up a panel in 1989 to look at the employment of disabled people. A significant number of countries prepared papers describing their policies and practices under agreed headings including one concerned with young people. The analysis of this material showed that most attention was being given to adult disability and rehabilitation. The sections on youth entry to work were weak and limited. There were, however, some very positive statements from some countries. If national authorities are not giving much attention to this issue it is not surprising that opportunities are limited.

Entering Employment

Obtaining employment is influenced by a range of characteristics embodied in the concept of employability. The perceptions of professionals and employers of the employability of disabled young people are all too often uninformed and superficial.

Young people who seek employment are helped if they are among other things (FEU, 1989c):

- reliable;
- conscientious;
- responsible;
- motivated to work;
- able to relate to colleagues;
- able to get to and from work;
- able to understand and carry out instructions;
- have acceptable standards of personal hygiene and self-presentation.

Quite apart from the personal characteristics that may limit employment chances there are a large number of external barriers such as difficulties in travelling, inaccessible premises, poor preparation and lack of support in the early stages of work.

In the absence of direct experience many myths and misconceptions about the employment potential of disabled young people are evident. These myths have been exposed as untrue by the experiences of major employers in the USA where, as discussed in Chapter 8, meticulously planned training programmes often prepare young people with severe disabilities for specific employment opportunities. Disabled employees have been found, for example, to have less time off for illness, fewer accidents and be better time keepers than other workers.

TECs are being urged to develop a common approach to disability in partnership with other agencies. A recent publication (*Business in the Community*, 1990) recognizes the potential of disabled young people, identifies barriers to their employment and sets out objectives, the means of achieving them and the actions it urges Councils to take.

Varieties of Employment

Activity, Training, Day and Social Education Centres

A variety of names has been given to centres for those with severe disabilities. There has usually been an element of work in their programmes. In the early years this work was undemanding, trivially rewarded with no likelihood of progression to, or training for, sheltered or open employment. There was a feeling that this was the client's level for life. More recently centres have sought work in the community and developed programmes with a greater sense of purpose and reality. The objective of supported open employment, however, is still not very common.

Sheltered Workshops

These have been one of the main ways of providing settled long-term employment for disabled people. Such workshops have provided few opportunities for advancement and very limited opportunities to enter open employment.

Output is subsidized but in recent years there has been greater emphasis on commercial objectives and attempts to maximize output and profitability. This has been particularly evident in Sweden and the USA. The result has been the employment of a greater percentage of socially handicapped persons with problems such as alcohol and drug abuse and an unwillingness to employ people with severe disabilities. The most proficient workers have been retained, to maintain production, and have not been introduced to open employment.

If sheltered work was ever seen as a means of entry to open employment, research in the USA has shown it to fail. There is no evidence that a period in sheltered work facilitates entry to work for young school leavers.

Open Employment

There are two intermediate variants of open employment which are now seen as more effective for many people with disabilities, the enclave and supported employment.

The *enclave* is a system where a group of individuals with disabilities work in a specially adapted area in an industrial or commercial enterprise. They are socially integrated and have access to all facilities available to other employees. The special nature of the approach rests in the adaptation of the immediate working environment.

Supported Employment

This is an approach in which the risk to the employer is reduced in a number of ways. The supporting agency provides on-site training and support and guarantees that the job will be done. The job is also subsidized for a period, often the first year, on the understanding that the employer assumes responsibility for payment if his experience is satisfactory.

In Genoa, Italy (Gerry, 1989), jobs are often tailor made with the agreement of employers, and support is provided by a social/health services team. There are two other approaches common in the USA. One involves the voluntary agency in training. A member of staff finds jobs, recruits workers and supports individuals placed in employment. The employer is guaranteed a worker, and if one individual proves unsatisfactory another is found. In this approach a fellow worker is recruited to provide day-to-day support although the agency worker is always on call.

The second approach (Hardman, 1988) involves a *job coach* responsible for the on-site training of individuals placed in open employment. The coaches ensure that the job is done even if, in the first stages, they have to complete the work themselves. Support is withdrawn when not necessary but the coach continues to be available to the employer if problems arise or retraining becomes necessary.

Financial Support

There are a number of ways in which governments support disabled people in employment. These are mostly designed for those disabled in adulthood.

Employment Subsidies

It is also common to find schemes that are based on the productivity of the disabled individual. These arrangements involve assessing the individual's output or level of proficiency as a percentage of the average. The employer pays for the level of proficiency and the individual's wages are made up to the average level by government subsidies. This kind of support can be given in enclaves, in supported employment and in open employment.

Modifying the Workplace

Allowances are available to modify the workplace of a disabled individual. This scheme is of more benefit to those disabled later in life and who have established an employment credibility. ess easy for young people to be supported by such schemes since e faced with a 'Catch 22' situation in which the equipment they need for training can only be obtained when they have a job. Again the system is designed for adults with skills who are disabled at work.

Disabled Work Allowance

The government is introducing a new benefit in current legislation. Its details are not yet known but it is said to meet some of the extra costs of working which disabled people face.

Employer Attitudes

The attitudes of employers to disability and their experience of workers with disabilities are crucial factors in obtaining a job. In the USA many employers have been active in recruiting those who are disabled. Others have responded to legislation which requires all recipients of government contracts to have a reasonable record of employing them. In the UK there is clear evidence of responsibility to existing employees who become disabled but much less evidence of the recruitment of those leaving education.

It is also generally true that private employers in all countries have a better record in this respect than national and local government and public authorities. However, even where multi-national businesses such as IBM, MacDonalds and Marriott have good records in the USA their UK arms show less evidence of similar activity.

Employer attitudes are affected by positive experiences. An important element in successful experience is the feeling of being supported. The initiatives that result in greater employment opportunities have two things in common:

1. There is always somebody on call to discuss problems and often to ensure that work is completed.
2. There are arrangements to pay the wages of the worker in full or in part for the first year.

In the case of job coaches the support is regularly present at work until acceptable levels of competence are achieved.

In other cases the agency replaces the worker to ensure the work is done. When the employer assumes responsibility for wages there may be a decreasing level of subsidy as competence is ensured. Shared risk and successful experience are potent influences on employer attitude.

Employment Issues

Although it is now clear that most young people want to work and that any wage they receive, however subsidized, is a positive gain for the exchequer, there are a number of issues to be considered.

The first is the degree of choice available to individuals. Should they have the choice not to work? A lot depends on the current values of society. If other young people are not given the choice should those with disabilities expect it? Perhaps a more difficult issue is the question of part-time or spasmodic work. Some individuals cannot sustain full-time employment. Others have good periods when they can work and periods when their condition makes it impossible. Flexible systems are needed involving both employment at home and elsewhere which takes these aspects into account.

A more potent issue is that of pensions and benefits. Regulations often require that supporting allowances are given up when employed and make it difficult to regain benefits when unemployed or unable to work. In some cases families have become used to the income derived from their child's disability allowances and see it as their entitlement for providing care. They may actively discourage both living independently and working because it reduces the family income.

Finally much employment for those with disabilities is low paid, often with little opportunity for advancement through further training, experience and increased competence. Active steps need to be taken to provide useful and worthwhile work. Experience has shown it is available even in time of high unemployment. It remains important to establish the worker with a disability as a worker entitled to the same conditions as others.

Independent Living

Discussion of the curriculum in school and further and continuing education have already shown independence to be an important outcome of education. It is equally important for social and employment services to continue to promote autonomy through further training and the ways in which they give individual support.

The possibilities for independent living that are available to young people with disabilities as they complete their transition are varied. The problems they face are sometimes difficult to surmount. The main question to be answered is whether they have the same opportunities as their contemporaries.

Villages and small communities, such as the Home Farm Trust provide, are a half-way house between the traditional institution and the community for many young people. They have a more adult regime and provide real work. In some organizations attempts to move individuals into the community: for example, by setting up cafés, restaurants and community shops. But many are still relatively isolated from their neighbours. Nevertheless, they give parents a security they do not always find in health and social service provision.

Family patterns have changed with smaller nuclear groups and different patterns of adult relationships. Many young people continue to live at home until they are married and separately housed. They establish their independence in their life at work and outside the home through economic independence. Others feel they must leave home to establish their own life style.

For most young people with marked disabilities the opportunities for independent living are much more difficult to realize. Living at home may result in continued dependent care with few opportunities to learn independent living skills. They cannot walk out, without help, to establish their own independent lives. If parents are not unwittingly putting on the breaks, professionals often do so – particularly when resources and alternatives are limited.

Establishing Independence

Establishing independence both in the family home and elsewhere is a process to which many of the transition partners can contribute. Although social service personnel must take the lead, colleges, the youth service (FEU, 1989f) and adult education (FEU, 1987b) all have important contributions to make. Joint planning will also be an advantage. The requirements for independence are:

- realism often provided by planned residential experience;
- a programme involving training, weaning and support;
- a shift of resources to the control of the individual;
- a recognition that achieving independence is a process that takes time and is never entirely complete;
- programmes can never be of finite length as individual needs vary;
- many individuals with profound and complex disabilities will need support for long periods but the nature of this should change so that the individual increasingly controls the form and timing of his own support.

Parents often need considerable help if they are to enable their children to establish independence as Wertheimer has shown (FEU, 1989c). Professionals and services do not always recognize their needs. Parents require time to think through their children's future and to gain confidence in their children's abilities to look after more and more parts of their lives.

The barriers are formidable. Parents may have got into the habit of dependent care and cannot let go. They may not trust, with justification, in many instances, local professionals and services. They may wish to limit risk taking and go for sheltered care. This is an area where professionals and services must recognize that developing independence is not just a matter of working with young people. Their children's growing self-advocacy and independence may be uncomfortable for many parents and professionals who need preparation for it and support during its development.

Conclusion

This chapter has looked at the third phase of transition where the outcomes of all the earlier planning and preparation are seen. The third phase is often the one that individuals are expected to manage themselves. Provision and services have an uncomfortable habit of disappearing after childhood. Administrators and professionals then expect sudden and complete adult competence. For many individuals, including those considered in this book, support and further training in the early years of employment and independent living is critical to their long-term quality of life.

PART III

CHAPTER 8

Initiatives and Innovations

Initiatives have been mentioned in previous chapters but it may be helpful to describe some at greater length. Examples set out in this chapter show that high expectations and effective education, training and support services lead to an independent working life even for young people with severe disabilities and learning difficulties. Although examples from other countries cannot be translated directly to this country, the essential ingredients of practices can be adopted.

A particular feature of initiatives in the USA is the contribution of universities. With the help of Federal and State grants many of them mount demonstration projects in schools and in the community. Such initiatives provide rigour in planning, execution and evaluation and also disseminate good practice through in-service education carried out by universities. Universities in the UK support few initiatives in special education and few in the field of further education.

The Final School Years

Two important elements in the final school years are the individual transition programme and the school programme from which its first elements are fashioned. The examples quoted come from the USA where high schools cater for the vocational element found in further education in the UK. These schools provide education up to 18 or 19 for all students and up to 21 or 23 for disabled students.

The High School Programme

The pioneering work of Bellamy, Brown, Hardman, Sailor and Wehman, all university based, in the USA has demonstrated the importance of a well-structured high-school programme with the clear aims of employment and independent living. *The Local Comprehensive School* (Sailor *et al.*, 1989) gives details of school programmes. It sets out a systematic training programme for young people with severe disabilities – mainly young people with severe learning difficulties in this country – based on modified behavioural approaches. The programme starts in the early teens and takes students into real living and working situations.

There are a number of key elements in these programmes. Experiences in travelling, shopping and taking part in recreational activities in the community are carefully planned with clear behavioural objectives and criteria. Learning is done in real situations in the community. For example, learning to shop for groceries requires the teacher to construct a programme which includes the behaviours required in all the appropriate neighbourhood shops. The performance criteria for the skill will involve competent shopping for a planned list of purchases in any of the different kinds of shop in the neighbourhood.

Similarly, vocational preparation and work experience is carried out in real employment situations. Use is also made of situations within schools to learn social and work skills. The same principles apply. Training reflects the range of employment in the neighbourhood. The programme provides experience in that range of work and at the same time concentrates on common aspects of employability such as interpersonal relationships and reliability.

Other important characteristics are developing personal decision making and choice, parental involvement in agreeing aims for programmes and continuous interaction with non-disabled contemporaries. Above all preparation at this stage becomes essentially local. There are no national or state curricula or criteria. The staff of high schools are expected to develop local networks and educate young people with severe degrees of disability to live and work in the community served by the school.

Such approaches can be found in the UK but most lack the rigorous task analysis, planning and evaluation provided by university personnel which is usually required in the USA.

The Individual Transition Plan

The Individual Education Plan (IEP) is a central feature of special education in the USA. An Individual Transition Plan (ITP) is now being introduced to address transition needs at the end of the school period. The purpose of such plans is to co-ordinate the contributions of different agencies towards agreed transition goals which have been planned with young people and their families. The features of such plans and examples of them can be found in Wehman and Sailor (Wehman *et al.*, 1988; Sailor *et al.*, 1989).

The ITP is initiated in the high school. It is up to the staff of schools to involve other agencies and to plan the handing over of responsibilities to them. Although conditions are different in the UK, it would be a step forward if schools recognized the need to initiate ITPs. The responsibilities of schools should not cease before they have prepared an ITP, completed its first stage and ensured that responsibilities for the next stage are clearly defined and accepted.

The stages in preparing and carrying out an individual transition plan are:

- Identifying team members – the student, his family, and counsellors or advocates for the student, school personnel and the appropriate personnel from other post-school agencies.
- Arranging meetings of team members with clear target dates.
- Developing the plan at the meetings with clearly defined agency responsibilities for its elements and a gradual transfer of responsibility from the school to other agencies.
- Implementing the plan and arranging review meetings to revise the plan at regular intervals (six months to a year).
- Setting up communications between ITP teams to look at local co-operation and collaboration.

All the information about who is involved, what is to be done by whom by when and the outcome is recorded in a standard form which is continually updated.

A Personal Guide or Point of Reference

Because of the variety and confusion of possibilities and responsibilities during transition the need for a guide for young people and their families has been widely recognized. The Warnock Report's (HMSO, 1978) 'named person' was one suggestion. OECD/CERI has been looking at examples in Member countries and has produced a study, *Disabled Youth: From School to Work* (OECD, 1991). One of these examples, the Kurator system in Denmark, has received considerable attention.

Special education is provided in Denmark in two main ways. Considerable efforts are made to meet needs in folkschools which are all age 6–16 schools run by municipalities (townships and their environs). Pupils with severe degrees of special need, about 1 per cent of the total, are educated in special schools run by county authorities. Both municipalities and counties get government grants for services.

The Kurator is a member of the school psychologist's team in each folk-school who teaches children with special educational needs and is responsible for their careers education and work experience. A Kurator is similar to a specialist careers teacher with additional contributions to make after school.

He or she has a number of non-teaching hours for work with young people and their families after they leave school and to form links with social services and employers. Support can be offered for up to four years after school. The Kurator is a facilitator who in the post-school period makes a contribution when requested to do so by young people and their families. Young people and families also have social workers who are primarily responsible for benefits and the family's social welfare problems.

The ways in which Kurators work and the time they have available varies from municipality to municipality. They began their work with young people with moderate learning difficulties in regular schools and are now extending it to all pupils with special educational needs in those schools.

There are tensions between counties and municipalities about responsibilities for individuals and the continuity provided by the Kurator is not available to all. However, the system is being supported and developed by the Danish Ministry of Education.

Further Education and Training

Developments in the UK have been patchy. The provision at the North Nottinghamshire College and the experimental work on transition are already on record (FEU, 1986) and there are many lessons still to be learned from that experience. Other, interesting initiatives in the UK have included TVEI where schools and colleges have worked together towards common objectives. Developments for blind students in the midlands and a project for people with physical disabilities in Scotland are other examples.

Support for Visually Impaired Students (Royal National Institute for the Blind, 1989)

When the RNIB closed its vocational college in the London area it was decided to establish a new institution next to other post-16 educational facilities. The college was built on a site adjacent to the university, a college of further education and a college of art.

The vocational college introduced a new concept of integration. It is the only example in the country of a specialist voluntary college offering residential and day courses in partnership with a maintained college. Visually impaired students are recruited from all over the UK. The college offers residential accommodation in the local community and accepts both school leavers and adults. The college also provides for students supported by employment training schemes and by local education authorities. The vocational college offers a range of in-house courses in commercial skills along the lines of those offered in the original college.

However, its main aim is to open up to visually impaired students the wider range of opportunities offered on the site. The college supports integrated students by providing material in braille, large print or on tape, diagrams in enlarged or tactile forms, specialist tuition and the allocation of a support tutor. Support is offered at three levels depending on the time (3–10 hours per week) and on the resources involved. Mobility training can be provided as part of this support as can training on a range of equipment designed to enable visually impaired students to 'read' ordinary print and store and retrieve information using micro-computers. As students become established and require less support the fees charged by the vocational college are reduced.

Students attending the college of further education may receive individual support in practical subjects and in tutorials where tutors from both institutions work together. The vocational college also offers a consultant outreach service to enable students to follow courses at other colleges near their own homes.

In the short time it has been established integrated provision has increased. The vice-principal of the further education college has a responsibility for liaison with the vocational college. The vocational college has been providing in-service training for the further education college staff and that college has provided a room in the business studies area for specialized equipment. Vocational college students are also full members of the Students Union of the further education college. This initiative provides a good example of specialist and non-specialist provision on adjacent sites and of the effective development of integrated opportunities through joint working and appropriate support.

Physical Disabilities (Stevenson College, 1991)

In a further education college, on the outskirts of Edinburgh in Scotland, students are supported by very specialized services to enable them to come to terms with their disabilities and to prepare for appropriate employment opportunities. The project, financed by a three year grant from the European Social Fund, was set up to provide integrated assessment, vocational guidance and training, work experience and job placements for young people and adults whose physical disabilities prevent them immediately joining regular courses.

Students have been involved in a number of transitions as a result of illness accident and long-term unemployment. The grant has enabled a unit to be set up and provided for the modification of premises and equipment and staffing. At the end of the grant the LEA recognized the value of the unit and continued its funding. The unit serves the immediate locality and the region.

A strong and significant element in the project has been the steering group where all the necessary professionals and employers have been instrumental in identifying appropriate jobs and the training needs involved. These are, at present, basic office skills, clerical, secretarial and computer skills. A suite of rooms was prepared for these purposes using standard equipment capable of flexible use and compatible with that used elsewhere in the college. The unit is situated on a busy corridor within the college and includes welfare and counselling facilities.

The key factor in selecting students is their motivation for employment. A multi-disciplinary assessment follows, involving all concerned with the project, and an individual curriculum is planned. All students start their programme within the unit but as soon as possible they move out to be supported on other college courses. The unit is likely to develop into a support unit which prepares students for regular courses throughout the college and continues to give them any necessary support.

The strong, sensitive staff team has demonstrated the ability to help students, for whom no other educational provision existed. It has helped them to acquire necessary basic learning skills, to complete vocational preparation and to develop as autonomous individuals.

Some students have found employment but others have been enabled to enrol on other regular courses. Many have been helped to come to terms with themselves and through self-assessment to establish the limits of their capacity to work. However, initially, employment opportunities have been limited mainly due to the reluctance of employers to adapt their working practices to meet student needs. But opportunities are beginning to improve as relationships are built up.

Access Centres

Sixteen centres have been established in colleges of further education and elsewhere. Their purpose is to assess the technological support that individual students might need to gain access to their chosen curriculum in the college they wish to attend. Most Access Centres serve a region but others have a specialist function in respect of particular disabilities. All centres are linked informally to enable staff to meet regularly, exchange information and update their knowledge and skills.

The centres carry a wider range of equipment than that of most colleges and have staff able to assess the needs of individuals. Students requiring help can visit centres or be seen in their own colleges. Once the problem of access to the curriculum has been identified initiatives are taken to overcome the problem by the use of appropriate technology. This may require individual adaptations, and some centres are staffed with technicians able to make them. Colleges can buy the consultancy services from centres when necessary. Access Centres are important elements in meeting student special needs and in extending the range of further education, training and employment opportunities available to disabled students.

The experiences of staff and students using technology in further education have been collected and analysed by Tom Vincent (1989) and the study both illustrates the positive benefits of good assessment and the appropriate use of technology. It also raises important issues which need to be faced if positive experiences in colleges are not to be followed by disillusionment and neglect in employment and independent living.

Entering Employment

Supported Employment

One of the most significant developments has been the increasing open employment of young people with severe disabilities, particularly severe intellectual disabilities. Research in the USA has shown the inadequacy of the sheltered workshop model where commercial objectives limit access for those with severe disabilities and where transfer to open employment is very limited. Supported open employment is much more successful. In Italy the Genoa approach is an outstanding example identified by OECD (Gerry, 1989). Other initiatives in the USA are also of interest (Hardman, 1988).

Genoa

The Genoa experience represents a genuine community response. Young people are placed in open employment and trained and supported by social service teams. The initiative was helped by the combination of a favourable political climate and the insight and drive of a local psychiatrist. Associations of employers and employees supported the employment of more disabled people in the community. Local health service personnel were also active in developing the initiative.

Young people with disabilities receive some preparation but the main strength of the scheme is the careful identification of jobs which individuals with severe disabilities can carry out. Each job is negotiated with the employer and associated workers. Both interests are assured of the ready availability of the support teams. The daily support of co-workers is an important element in the programme.

Another important factor is that the state, region and municipality combine to pay the young person's wage for the first year. Thereafter the employer accepts responsibility. Support teams continue to work with employers and fellow workers in a training programme and are also on call if there are problems.

The results to date have been impressive. In a city with 12 per cent unemployment, 400 recent placements have resulted in an over 90 per cent job retention rate after the first three years of employment. The scheme has now been extended to other cities.

The Sheltered Placement Scheme

The Shaw Trust administers one form of the sheltered placement scheme. This scheme is designed for registered disabled people to enable them to work at their own capacity. It involves a host firm, a sponsor and the Training Agency (now the TEED). The host firm provides work. There is a contract for services between the sponsor and the host firm whereby the services of the disabled person are made available to the firm for an agreed payment based on the individual's percentage of normal productivity. If the agreement is endorsed by the TA the sponsoring organization receives a grant to subsidize the percentage wage paid by the employer.

The Shaw Trust is an organization which aims to promote the social and economic integration of those who are disabled by means of permanent employment. It provides training programmes and homeworking. Among its many activities is the support of more than 1000 individuals in the DE's sheltered placement scheme.

The sheltered placement scheme is threatened by limits being placed on finance as resources are diverted from providers to TEC's.

Independent Living

Many organizations provide sheltered independent living in villages and small communities. Independent living in the community is more risky for parents and is resisted by neighbours in many areas. To be successful it requires sustained training and support by social service personnel for which resources are not usually available. This uncertainty of support is a major reason for the unpopularity of small communities with parents.

There are now a wide range of programmes which support independent living. In this country voluntary organizations are actively developing individual accommodation designed to facilitate it. Among them the John Groom Society has been particularly active.

Another initiative has been taken by the Shaftesbury Society in collaboration with a college of further education. The Society runs two hostels for people with physical disabilities adjacent to the college. One of them is for students who wish to attend the college but the majority of residents at the other also attend some classes.

This provision facilitates independent living and learning and is a good example of what can be achieved by co-operation between voluntary and statutory organizations.

Conclusion

Each service and each local area will need to plan arrangements to suit the needs and conditions which exist. It is important to reiterate that examples of innovations can only stimulate thinking. A number of features can be identified. Most, if not all, successful initiatives are local. A strong supportive local network is essential. Careful inter-agency planning is another feature.

The initiatives in this chapter are intended to give some practical examples of the ways in which the principles being enunciated in this book can be put into practice where there is a will to do so.

CHAPTER 9

Major Transition Issues

Preceding chapters have looked at each of the three stages of transition and at interesting practices. It is now possible to look at the transition phase and process as a whole and discuss major issues that need consideration. The purpose of this chapter is to look at:

1. The contributions of all the professionals and how they might be changed to support effective transition.
2. The criteria by which to judge whether a transition programme is effective.

Partners in Transition

A long list of potential contributors was set out earlier. Some of their contributions have been discussed. While looking at each sector separately it is assumed that effective inter-agency co-operation should also be addressed. The central questions are whether all professionals:

- Have agreed objectives for transition which are compatible.
- Are working together to implement individual programmes.
- Are facilitating progress towards an independent adult working life.
- Have agreed criteria for evaluating individual progress.

Education

Education Officers

In the immediate future officers for schools and further education should have a clear concept of transition and work together to ensure continuity between schools and colleges. Developing this continuity should also include the contributions of adult education and the youth service. However, new legislation will place greater responsibilities on schools and colleges. Close relationships and working arrangements with officers of other services, particularly social and health services, should be built in to job descriptions. This is not just necessary for young people with disabilities and learning difficulties since all young people will profit from greater continuity and coherence between phases of education.

Advisors and Inspectors

As with officers there is a tendency for advisors and inspectors to work narrowly within either the school or further education sectors. Not only do they need to work across phases but they also need to set their contribution within a context of other local authority services. It is intended that as independent assessors they should play an increasingly important role in the quality control of education and of transitional arrangements as individuals leave the education sector.

Secondary and Special School Teachers

Secondary and special school teachers need to develop a wide concept of transition which recognizes the importance of the next stage of further education and training. Apart from subject specialists both *special needs co-ordinators* and *careers teachers* have a particular contribution to make. They must know what is on offer at the end of the school period and prepare pupils with special needs for that stage. Careers teachers, working closely with careers officers, should also be a source of information and guidance about the opportunities available to all school leavers including those with special needs.

Educational Psychology Services

These are often very influential in the assessment of individual needs. However, many psychologists confine their work to the school period and have little time to give in the post-school period. If psychologists are to make a realistic contribution to transition plans they must be well informed about the post-school period and provide support to further and continuing education staff.

Careers Officers

Careers officers with both general and specialist duties, will have to revise their approaches in the future as education and training for all becomes a reality. If they are to continue to work in schools the careers service will have to be well informed about post-school opportunities. Careers officers will also need to work much more closely with colleges and concentrate on post-18 employment opportunities. Specialist careers officers in particular may well be an important point of reference for individuals with disabilities and learning difficulties during transition. The nature of their work will need to change to take in new developments. The employment objective for all should occasion a more positive approach to work for those with severe and complex disabilities.

Further Education College Staff

Both subject and special needs staff will need to be conversant with their student's school experiences and with school curricula. They will also need to be equally familiar with the opportunities available to students after they have completed their programmes in college. Staff will need to look both ways and fit their vital bridging contribution into individual transition programmes.

Social Services

Both the Disabled Persons Act (1986) and the Children Act (1989) give increased responsibilities to social services for the transition of young people classified as disabled. This together with new responsibilities for securing and inspecting provision made by others will require a much greater awareness of training programmes. Non-directive client centred negotiation will need to be supplemented by more active involvement in education and training programmes, often in co-operation with others.

Health Services

For many young people the therapies they receive in school cease when they leave. Health care transition is badly managed. It is not simply a matter of resources, although these are important. It involves a sudden switch from school-focused services to a personal search for particular elements of service. It is much more a question of continuity between child and adult services. Are health service personnel aware of transition issues? Their contribution to effective arrangements where physical and sensory disabilities are concerned is vital.

Employment Services

In the past the disablement aspect of employment services was concentrated on disabilities resulting from accidents in adult life. There is still limited recognition of the importance of supporting the entry of young people with disabilities and learning difficulties to work. There is often little recognition that becoming employable takes time and requires work experience. Decisions taken before such experience can themselves be handicapping. Disablement resettlement officers have an important part to play in transitions.

The setting up of TECs to respond to and prepare for local labour needs could be a new opportunity to provide for disadvantaged groups. Resources going to them are limiting funds available for special programmes and for wage supplements. What steps can be taken to ensure that councils meet the needs of all and not just of the easy to train and place? Staff of TECs must be aware of transition issues and of the potential of those with special needs. The work of councils should be judged on their support for transition as a whole and for an adequate range of provision not on high levels of success in narrowly defined areas.

Voluntary Organizations

The contributions of the large number of voluntary organizations vary widely. While some have been pioneers in promoting independence and employment, others appear to retain a vested interest in a dependent population. All need to face up to transition issues and promote good practices in vocational preparation and in living in the community. The involvement and formal and informal support of parents is a particular contribution which they can make.

Local authorities have not always been very good at working with voluntary organizations nor have organizations always had effective local branches. Nevertheless, this co-operation can be vital during transition, and workers in both sectors need to explore new ways of working together.

Parents

The Warnock Report (HMSO, 1978) promoted the partnership of parents in special education. Their contribution to children's growth and development is paramount and needs to be understood and recognized by all professionals. The contribution of parents to transition merits much greater space than is possible in this book, particularly the difficulties faced by some families, such as nuclear and single-parent families, in supporting their childrens' transition.

It is important to discuss both the contributions and needs of parents during this phase because they are not always receiving adequate attention. Recent work by Wertheimer (FEU 1989c) and Clare (1990) has shown that many parents of young people with severe disabilities have great difficulty in allowing their children to take risks and become more adult.

The transition phase is a crucial time for reappraising and readjusting parent/professional/young people relationships. Skilled help may be necessary but above all the three contributors to the relationships have to display informed sensitivity if long-term adult bonds are to be formed.

Criteria

Having looked at the contributing partners we now turn to the ways in which they plan and manage transition. The criteria set out do not provide answers but they do provide a check-list. They may be used:

1. To evaluate provision.
2. To assess the progress of individuals.

Evaluating provision involves looking at facilities and services in a particular area, at the options and choices available to all young people and those available to individuals considered to be handicapped. Evaluation also involves looking at the ways schools, colleges, LEAs, social services, employment services, health services and a wide range of voluntary organizations make their contributions and co-operate towards agreed ends. The performance outcomes of a wide variety of programmes and practices must be assessed.

The criteria listed are not complete. Most people will wish to add to them. The ones which follow have been chosen to draw attention to crucial aspects of transition and to some of the most important barriers to be overcome on the way to adulthood.

Assessment

Assessment and self-assessment are natural human activities which form part of social interaction. From the early years children weigh each other up in different situations. Most have a choice of areas in which to compete but those with disabilities are 'handicapped'.

In most complex societies assessment has increased in importance for many reasons concerned with the reward of effort and the support of inadequacy. Examining educational achievements is one of the most common forms with high standards affording entry to higher education and limited achievements leading to special help. Assessment is also the means of deciding who is qualified in professional and employment terms as well as who is handicapped and who receives various pensions and benefits.

Assessment and the use to which it is put are important issues. Procedures are only as good as the questions they are asked to answer. For example, assessment arrangements designed to identify learning difficulties in school may be inappropriate for identifying transitional needs. A procedure designed to see whether a person does or does not fall within a category of handicap may be useless as a basis for developing an individual programme.

Young adolescents weigh up their attributes and deficits within their peer group during the secondary school period. They may not use the same criteria as schools but their assessments are powerful determinants of individual self-confidence and social status. It is during adolescence that the long-term implications of disabilities make a renewed impact on young people. They may become depressed as a result of this reappraisal. Without sensitive support it may be much more difficult for them to accomplish a positive and forward looking self-assessment.

Self-assessment is obviously influenced by adult opinions and attitudes. Assessment in the final school years should be a process shared by young people. This sharing should include the reasons for assessment, its objectives and the methods to be used as well as the outcomes. Assessment should also prepare individuals to negotiate their individual learning needs in self-assessment procedures in further education and employment. An individual transition plan will be useless if it is based solely on performance in school. It must also be based on behaviour in social and employment situations and take into account individual preferences. The ability to live independently can only be judged from experiences of living in a domestic situation without constant parental care. The ability to be employed can similarly only be judged by work experience on real work sites.

Assessment should have been continuous during the school years primarily to help teachers plan their work. In the final years of schooling it should be designed to produce an individual transition plan and identify what the final school years should contribute to it. Such assessment should be multi-disciplinary and begin to make clear the responsibilities of the services and agencies which are to contribute to the plan. Assessment at this stage should also provide some of the information a young person with a disability or learning difficulty needs to make decisions and choices about future education and training.

There is now a legal basis for individual assessment towards the end of the school period. If that assessment is used to categorize, if school performance is used to decide what individuals can or cannot do in other situations and if the result is to limit choices and options this assessment may be handicapping. What is required is positive assessment, which includes evaluating performance in real-life situations outside school, and which identifies individual transition needs.

Information About and Knowledge of the System

Most young people and their parents only know the facilities and services which they are using at the time. Few have knowledge of the whole range of what is or should be available. Because of the fragmentary nature of responsibilities and services in most places it is very difficult for young people and their families to get a clear and accurate picture of all the options available to them. Young people and their parents may have to search for it. Information about all the agencies and services with a potential to contribute to transition is not often readily available in a coherent form.

Its provision should be part of the teaching programme in the final school years and part of the preparation of parents for transition. A few local authorities have produced useful publications. Others have supported voluntary organizations and parents groups. The Newham Parents Centre is a very effective example. The comprehensiveness, relevance and clarity of available information is thus an important criterion of effective transition arrangements.

The Nature of the Transition Programme

A narrow sector or professional concept of transition may result in a lack of balance in programmes of activities. They may not give equal weight to all the major aims already set out. There may be an over emphasis on independence and no real belief in the possibility of employment. It is particularly important to keep an open mind and provide an appropriately balanced programme at the beginning of the process of transition.

A number of questions must be asked about the curriculum in the final school years and in further education:

- What is the balance between providing knowledge of life after school and developing the skills necessary to live it?
- Are there opportunities to discuss disability issues?

Do the young person's opportunities, experiences and training possibilities achieve a reasonable balance between preparation for work, for independence, for community participation and for an adult family life?

Participation, Autonomy and Self-advocacy

Personal autonomy for those who are disabled is not just a quality of life but a human right. The expectations of parents and professionals have a crucial influence on the personal aspirations of the individual young person. Do facilities and services lead to young people having choices and managing their own lives?

The transition phase should involve a major restructuring of professional and parental attitudes to and relationships with disabled young people, as Clare has shown (1990), if they are to achieve a positive self-concept and manage their own lives to the maximum extent. Opportunities to discuss personal disabilities and attitudes to and feeling about them are essential. Self-presentation and self-advocacy are essential ingredients in transition programmes.

In all the stages, when moving from school to adult and working life there should be opportunities to develop choice. There should be similar opportunities to acquire the skills and participate in decision making. An effective programme should result in young people being capable of managing many areas of their lives.

However, where progress towards autonomy is slow or self-presentation continues to be difficult the transition programme should ensure that the individual has available an advocate. Those who act in this capacity should represent the individual's wishes and views. Parents and professionals may not always be sufficiently detached to do so. It has to be recognized that some families and parents are not in a position to provide adequate support during transition. In that case the ITP should include provision for a substitute advocate for their children.

Financial Arrangements

Are resources always channelled through professionals and parents or does the young person gradually gain control over them? This is not just a transition issue. Professional management of the lives of adults defined as handicapped has been traditional with resources only made available by professionals through agencies.

Disabled adults have had to fight to manage their own lives particularly in respect of finance. How do transitional arrangements deal with this issue? An important criterion of effectiveness should be that at the end of transition most young people with disabilities should be able to take some responsibility for managing their own time and resources.

How are Families Involved?

Professionals working with adolescents tend to concentrate their efforts on developing the independence of the young people with whom they work. They may inform parents about programmes but they do not always provide sustained opportunities for discussion. The involvement of parents and families in the care and management of young people with disabilities is continuous. They need opportunities to discuss programme objectives, their anxieties about their children's future and their attitudes to an adult life for them as Wertheimer has shown (FEU, 1989c). The need for care may inhibit parents from considering their children's independence. There are profound emotional issues not often responsive to information and reason. The subsequent nature of parental and family relationships and involvement is thus an important criterion of effectiveness of professional work.

Young people may find a dependent relationship, based on necessary physical care, an impressive barrier to independence and adulthood. The development of a new relationship between parents, professionals and an emerging adult with a disability is a delicate process which will not always occur spontaneously. Sensitive and practical help will often be necessary to reconsider relationships and form more adult ones. Parental and professional relationships with young people are a significant indicator of the effectiveness of transitional arrangements.

What are Service Priorities?

Professionals have traditionally given a slightly paternalistic charitable service. They have believed that they know what disabled people need. It cannot always be said that the interests of the disabled have been paramount. Some facilities and services appear to have been organized for the convenience of the professionals rather than clients.

One of the major questions to be asked is, do professionals really want independent adults with minds of their own? Is a decently grateful dependence more comfortable to live with? It has been common practice for individuals to be put into categories of handicap and assumed to have the same needs as others with the same disability. Young people may be treated as stereotypes and fitted into available categorical programmes on a take it or leave it basis. It is still relatively uncommon to try to find out what individuals with profound learning difficulties would like.

How are professional, agency and service priorities decided? This is not simply a matter of having a stated policy. It is how agency staff carry out their work. Subtle nuances in practices may convey messages to clients. It has already been shown that growing independence and adult status require a greater equality in participation and decision making. Individuals need a personal plan; a changing pattern of professional practice, which recognizes that the disabled person as a responsible adult should be the hallmark of effective programmes. The extent to which facilities and services are flexible, change in response to individual need over time and respond to consumer demands is an important criterion.

Coherence and Progression

The last issues to be considered – continuity, coherence and progression – arise from the interaction of all the separate elements. They are therefore the hardest to achieve and evaluate.

Continuity

As individuals move through transition discontinuities are common. Young people and their families may be handed over from one professional to another, and from one institution or agency to another; or, having been discharged from the responsibility of one, have to seek out another agency. These changes often take place without any recognition of common concerns and objectives.

One indicator of effective transition is the degree to which professionals and agencies know each other's work. Another is the extent to which curricula and training programmes are jointly planned or at least have common objectives. A third is the degree to which there is progression and a professional trust and a willingness to build on the work of others. Evidence of continuity from school to an adult working life is an important indicator of effective arrangements.

Coherence

It is argued that the approach to transition is commonly fragmented. Work skills, for example, are developed in isolation from social and life skills. Experience has shown that the specific skills required in particular jobs are often of considerably less importance than the social and life skills necessary to function effectively in a place of work. Participation in the community together with access to recreational and leisure activities depends on managing one's own resources, particularly those derived from paid employment, as well as on social skills. An independent life in a family or appropriate social group requires the status of a contributor as well as competence in the other areas of adult life.

Progression

Although implicit in the discussion of continuity and coherence it is important to stress the need for the individual to sense that he or she is making progress. The curriculum and the training programme should have successive goals as an individual moves through the three stages of transition. The individual transition plan together with a regular review of its implementation should ensure that progress is noted and encouraged.

Inter-agency Co-operation and Joint Planning

Continuity, coherence and progression in transitional arrangements require joint planning and inter-professional and inter-agency collaboration at national, regional and local levels. In practice few effective methods have evolved.

Those working in the field identify a number of characteristics as essential attributes of good inter-agency work. Some of them are necessary conditions for effective work. First and foremost there has to be pressure from consumers and voluntary organizations. Without it professionals may have no incentive to work with each other. The agencies involved have to make a commitment to work with others. Agencies must also develop a shared philosophy, for example about integration.

The tasks of different professionals and agencies need to be clearly specified and the time required for inter-agency work must be included in plans and job descriptions. Shared activities must have a specific focus and common goals together with a written agreement to implement inter-agency policy decisions.

There are obviously a number of barriers to collaboration. These include the different management styles and cultures of each agency, different planning cycles and time scales of work, the ownership of initiatives and of clients/students/customers. Other problems are a lack of time for co-operative ventures and the effects of service confidentiality and a consequent lack of shared information.

Effective inter-agency work requires the ability:

- to summarize and state a problem;
- to understand and speak the languages of other services and communicate effectively;
- to define realistic criteria for progression and objectives;
- to write agreements;
- to give and take in work with others together with self-awareness;
- to display appropriate behaviour and diplomacy;

- to capitalize on the unexpected;
- to manage co-ordination with contracting resources.

It is important to develop attitudes and strategies that are positive to inter-agency work and to enhance the individual skills necessary for such work more widely within agencies. Small inter-agency task oriented groups may be an important first step in developing more widespread co-operation. It is also important to disseminate good examples of collaboration, to value the contribution of others and to look at the process of collaboration as well as the outcomes.

Staff Development

If the numerous partners involved are to achieve the complex array of objectives for successful transition staff development will be necessary. This will be required both within the in-service programmes of different sectors but more importantly on an inter-agency basis. The focus of this book is transition, not professional development. But appropriate staff development is an important criterion of effective transitional arrangements (FEU, 1987c; FEU/Training Agency/Skill, 1989).

Final Outcomes – The Orientation

The criteria used to evaluate transitional arrangements can be considered in terms of their general orientation. The overall thrust of provision and services can be gauged by asking a number of general questions:

- Are policies and practices generally integrative or segregative in their implementation?
- Are practices oriented towards dependent care or independence?
- Do policies and practices recognize individuality and choice?
- Are policies and practices client oriented or heavily influenced by the interests of professional staff?
- Finally are practices inward looking within the agency or service or do they reach out to co-operate with other agencies?

Aims, criteria and orientation are interrelated as are continuity, coherence and progression. In attempting to set out a framework for a detailed review of transition policies and practices it is not intended to provide a blueprint. Each authority, each local area and each neighbourhood will have to consider transition and evolve a pattern of opportunities and choices from which to fashion individual transition plans.

CHAPTER 10

A Way Ahead

It will be increasingly vital to make use of the contributions of all young people through employment and independent functioning. This is an economic necessity. Coherent support for the transition of individuals with special needs will require co-ordinated efforts by all of the main agencies and professionals concerned. Up to now progress has been halting with little evidence of inter-agency planning for individuals whom it is known will be starting their transition.

This final chapter looks ahead and sets out an agenda for that reconsideration. It poses questions and indicates the kind of answers it hopes might be made.

Who is Responsible for Change and Development?

Each agency develops facilities and services for which it is responsible. Competition for resources and for separate budgets further strengthens separate development. Any agency attempting to take a lead in inter-agency co-operation, or inter-professional training, is liable to be seen as wanting to take overall responsibility rather than share it.

Who has responsibility for the development, co-ordination and evaluation of provision and services? It is seldom to be found at central government level although local authorities are urged to co-ordinate their activities with others.

It might be reasonable to expect universities and colleges of higher education to make a contribution. However, when one looks at where current developments spring from there is little evidence of activity in that sector. This is both true of the sector as a whole and also of preparation to work with students with disabilities and learning difficulties within it. The comparatively limited provision in higher education is almost all confined to the school phase.

Improved transitional arrangements depend on appropriate staff training and preparation. At present almost no attention is given to transition in the post-school period. Inter-professional training experiences are a prerequisite to inter-agency co-operation. Universities and colleges of higher education represent relatively neutral settings in which this can take place. Any of the relevant faculties could make a useful contribution.

Real progress is often initiated locally by individuals. Working together with others in a network supported by a local community can achieve real progress. A promising approach to inter-agency co-operation, adopted in one county is based on the formation of local networks. Professionals working in a particular town or area meet regularly. Where this is effective it provides regular opportunities for learning about each other's work and sharing solutions to common problems. It is essential that local authorities support such networks.

The Nature of Specialism

All facilities and services are affected by their approach to professional specialization. Specialization, in this context, may be in the needs of a specific disability or in meeting special needs in general. Provision to meet special needs must have discernible characteristics if it is to be funded. Staff with knowledge and experience of special needs may be one characteristic and a vital resource.

The issue is how best to make specialist contributions within integrated service provision. Two broad approaches can be discerned and both are matters of emphasis rather than of distinctly separate philosophies.

Generic improvers assume that all facilities can develop a capacity, thorough in-service education, good assessment, planning and management, to meet the needs of individuals with a wide range of different disabilities, styles and rates of learning. They tend to favour generic support services in integrated settings. Many also believe that the existence of separate special education and disability services is segrative.

Disability specialists are individuals who concentrate on the nature of different disabilities and the learning and other needs associated with them. They specialize in the technology, materials and methods of instruction most suited to individuals with a particular disability. Many also believe that separate provision and services for each kind of disability are essential.

A generic, general improvement approach does not always give sufficient weight to the specialist needs of individuals and the disability specialist approach often gives too little weight to needs common to all with disabilities and learning difficulties. While it is necessary for individuals to have access to specialist expertise about their particular disabilities and learning difficulties, it is equally necessary to meet the greatest possible number of common special needs through improvements in the education and through support services available to all. The cost to society of not doing so is prohibitive.

The two approaches are not mutually exclusive. The problem is to achieve the right balance. This is not an abstract issue since it bears directly on the allocation of resources. In educational terms the issue can be characterized by the difference between primary and secondary education approaches to subject specialization. In the primary schools curriculum specialists work with and through class teachers. They influence and support without a separate territory. In secondary schools there are separate departments or faculties for subject specialisms. Specialisms must have a separate territory.

It is far easier for those unfamiliar with the nature of the problem to apply simplistic solutions. This may result in a preference for separate schools, classes, courses and services and the use of individual specialists in a supporting capacity being seen as a luxury. Many believe that professionals must have a defined group of individuals for whom they are responsible. Separate and disability specific provision is often preferred as a basis on which to allocate resources.

The model used to resource provision for special needs will have an increasing influence on the development of facilities and services for transition. A separate territory model is divisive and resource intensive. A supportive generic model is fraught with interpersonal tensions and competing resource problems. Difficult decisions have to be made. These considerations apply both within services, such as education and to relationships between services.

The Education Contribution

For a brief period after the Education Act 1981 meeting special educational needs was high on the agenda of LEAs, institutions and services in all phases of education. Whether the best use was made of that period is questionable. However, there is a better awareness of the existence of special educational needs.

A number of LEAs, among them the ILEA (ILEA, 1985) and Gloucestershire, have carried out systematic reviews of their provision and services. These have shown the importance of looking at all phases of education. A longitudinal examination exposes discontuities and repetitions, gaps in responsibilities, the absence of regular co-operation with other service partners and the generally *ad hoc* nature of many arrangements. It is still true that few authorities have accurate information about the special education facilities and services they provide, what they actually do, how much they cost and whether resources are well used. A special education audit of all provision and services from the early years to adulthood is long overdue in many areas.

There is very little understanding of the most effective ways in which education systems, schools, colleges and other services can and should meet the range of special educational needs that exist. *What is Special Education?* (Fish, 1989) suggested a framework for discussion in the school sector.

LEAs should be asking themselves a number of questions about meeting special needs in further and continuing education. These include:

- How does the strategic plan for further and continuing education deal with meeting special needs?
- What kinds of provision will be recognized as meeting special needs?
- How will the authority work with TECs to ensure that the needs of all school leavers are met?

Colleges and other educational services should be asking:

- Do college development plans show how special needs are to be met?
- How can the range of work offered be made accessible to a wider range of students including those with disabilities and learning difficulties?
- What are the best uses of resources intended to support students with special needs?
- Is there a clear allocation of responsibility for special needs work?
- Are there arrangements for systematic co-operation with other agencies?
- Are there arrangements for evaluating the quality of the work?

Post-school education and training is a shared responsibility. Not only employers and employees but also vocational training staff, parents, social workers and other carers have an educational role. Education staff will need to work with others to develop shared programmes and curricula.

Many of the features of effective special education, such as individual programmes and the management of a wide variety of learning rates and styles, are becoming equally important in the mainstream of education and training, e.g. TVEI work. The future role of education is not confined to shared responsibility for students, particularly those in transition, but it also includes disseminating best practices to others involved in vocational and social education and training.

The introduction of individual training credits for school leavers will provide education and training with a new challenge. Unless the youth group has adequate guidance and counselling individuals may find choice difficult. Training credits may also limit the opportunities of those with special needs unless their value is enhanced to make the provision of good quality training attractive.

Social Service Contributions

New legislation has given greater responsibilities to social services departments for young people in transition and particularly those who are disabled. Better data about who is registered as disabled and about the costs and effectiveness of post-school alternatives will be required.

By the end of 1991 departments will have to develop individual transition plans for all those leaving care and will have to secure rather than provide many of the elements in them. This should lead to more inter-agency co-operation. The further learning of young people will need to be actively fostered with more emphasis on structured approaches to learning and less reliance on non-directive counselling.

Questions social services need to ask might include:

- Is there a policy for the transition of young people with disabilities from school to an adult working life?
- Is there a range of opportunities from which individual plans can be developed?
- Is there a clear allocation of responsibility for transition plans and for the inter-agency co-operation involved in their development?

Social services departments and social workers can undoubtedly ask themselves many more questions.

The Contribution of Employment Services

A heavy reliance is being placed on TECs to provide the framework for more effective vocational preparation. They will have the resources, they will be expected to know the local employment and unemployment situations and who needs training. Hopefully, they will recognize the importance to the labour market of disadvantaged and minority groups. There is a real danger that limited resources and the search for quick success will result in those who are easy to train getting priority and opportunities for the disabled, already limited by the diversion of funds from specialist agencies to TECs, being further restricted.

Among the questions to be addressed by TECs should be:

- Does the council have information about all the young people with disabilities who are leaving school?
- Does the council's programme include support for training for individuals with disabilities and special needs?
- Are there arrangements for inter-agency consultation and co-operation?
- Where there are experiments with training credits how are the needs of those who are disabled met?
- Is the endorsement policy working effectively?

It will be some time before the work of TECs, and in particular their contributions to the training of young people with disabilities, can be evaluated.

The Contributions of Other Services

One of the most noticeable features of health care is the way therapeutic services often fail to provide for young people after school. This is partly because the therapies are available in some school and local child health clinics but are then only available in adult hospital clinics. Transitional arrangements need greater attention where individuals with physical disabilities are dependent on them for the continued mobility and movement necessary for independent living and work. It is not proposed to list all the possible contributors but mention must be made of health services, leisure and recreation services, transport and housing.

The Contributions of Parents and Families

In all that has been written it has been assumed that parents and families are the major contributors to effective transition. It has also been recognized that in many instances they receive very little informed help once their children leave school. Parents of children who are disabled, like other parents, should be looking towards an adult life for them and helping to develop an individual plan for transition to it.

A Common Approach

Although education has been the strongest thread running through this book, transition is a shared business. The principal contributors have been identified. Familiarity with each other's contributions and with local planning procedures and local networks are essential elements in effective arrangements. A shared concept of transition leads to a number of common issues which all must address.

One of the most critical is shared professional training. In looking at the responsibilities of special needs specialists in the future it is assumed that they will apply to all the professionals concerned, not just those in education. The communality of the desired attributes would suggest that training opportunities, such as the multi-disciplinary degree course at Norwich City College, should become more widespread.

The Future Specialist

Standards of management, assessment and curriculum and service delivery for those with disabilities and learning difficulties must be the same as those applied to other work. This does not involve less care and compassion but combines traditional sensitivities with a special professionalism. The work of a specialist must have certain characteristics which have become clear from the effective work of special needs co-ordinators and advisers in regular schools and colleges, in social services and in employment services.

Qualities required for doing the job include:

- knowledge and experience of individuals with a disability and special knowledge of at least one major disability;
- understanding of the whole range of individual needs from mild degrees of disability to severe, profound and complex degrees;
- knowledge of the system in which they are employed and of recent legislation and regulations;
- knowledge of related local services and the legislation and regulations which apply to them;
- knowledge and ability to fit a contribution into an individual transition plan and a continuous curriculum coupled with an awareness of the previous and subsequent range of learning experiences offered;
- skills of observation and analysis which look at the problems of individuals and identify specific needs;
- the ability to devise with others individual programmes;
- good inter-personal skills to work individuals, their families and with colleagues in a wide range of agencies;

- good knowledge of the facility or service and ability to foster easy access to senior management and contribute to policy development;
- good management skills both of personal time and commitments and of staff and resources;
- the ability to monitor and evaluate one's own work and that of others.

This list could be extended and modified to suit local conditions but it gives the flavour of the difficult tasks facing a co-ordinator for work with individuals with disabilities and learning difficulties in a variety of settings.

It is also worth considering what the effects might be if representatives in all the major services were enabled to develop the characteristics set out above. It would seem most likely that mutual understanding and respect would increase and co-operation become easier.

Questions

There are a number of questions which all contributors need to ask themselves about transitional arrangements. Forms of provision and service convey messages to those who are handicapped. They are sensitive to implicit messages and suspicious of expressions of intent. Both the questions and the answers reveal attitudes and values which must be examined if equal quality in provision and equality of opportunity are to become a reality particularly during vital phases such as transition.

Department, Agency and Service Questions

They should be asking themselves:

- Is there a policy for meeting the needs of young people and adults with disabilities and learning difficulties?
- How will arrangements to meet their needs be included in strategic planning?
- Is there a recognition of a personal entitlement to the same opportunities as others?
- Is there a person with a defined responsibility in the department, agency or service for seeing that their needs are met?
- What kinds of provision is recognized as meeting these needs?
- Is there curriculum or programme from which individual transition plans can be developed?
- What criteria will they use to evaluate the quality of provision to meet these needs and of individual programmes?
- What steps are being taken to facilitate inter-service and inter-agency joint planning, provision, monitoring and professional training?

Questions for Professionals

They ask themselves:

• How best can they develop self-advocacy in their students/clients/
  trainees and shift power to them as adults?
• What steps can they take to develop close working arrangements with
  colleagues in other agencies to ensure effective and coherent plans for
  all individuals in transition and in particular with respect to those with
  disabilities and learning difficulties?

Questions for Families

They might ask themselves:

• What sort of adult life they hope their children will lead?
• What steps can they take to create the opportunities they want in their
  neighbourhoods?
• What can they do to help their children develop independence,
  employment skills and an adult life-style?

Questions for Young People

They might ask themselves:

• What information do they need to make informed choices?
• Who can help them to develop a life plan?
• What kind of support do they need?
• What would help them take more control of their lives?

Although the answers to these questions will be influenced by agency
priorities, local conditions and personal preferences, it is worth
emphasizing that few can be answered in isolation. Sectors and agency
approaches need to be compatible and they must be developed in co-
operation with young people and their families.

Conclusions

Many parents and professionals are currently concerned about the transition of young people with special needs from school to an adult working
life of value to the community. This book has attempted to provide a
framework within which to discuss the issues raised by that concern.

The aim has been to establish a concept of transition, particularly from
school to an adult working life, as a phase and a process requiring coher-

ence, continuity and progression. Although having a strong educational focus, stress has been placed on the need for all agencies to share in the implementation of individual transition plans.

Initiatives exist that show what is possible. They emphasize the importance of high expectations. Well-planned education and training can lead to greater independence and employment opportunities. Much work is necessary to develop a range of similar opportunities in this country.

One step that could be taken is the setting up of a small inter-departmental and inter-professional task group to develop guidelines for the transition of all young people, including those with disabilities and learning difficulties. Such a group should look at the financing of transition, within the framework of training credits and allowances, and the long-term costs of not doing so.

This should be followed by experimental initiatives linking the work of TEED, TECs, the DES and the new FE body to be set up. Jointly financed by the partners, the initiatives should be designed and evaluated by university or polytechnic departments. The evidence collected should be used as a basis for any necessary legislation and good practices should be disseminated.

It is not easy for individuals to influence policies and practices but a shared vision is a positive help. Such a vision is vital if young people are to get the opportunities they deserve and if educational investment in them is to be realized.

Bibliography

Business and Community Publications (1990):
  A Vision for TECs.
  Developing Good Practice – The TEC Special Training Needs Strategy.
  TECs Partnerships with Education.
  TECs and Disability – Action Issues.
  TECs: Customised Training and Targetted Recruitment.
Available from Business in the Community, 227a City Road, London EC1V 1LX.
CBI (1989). *Towards a Skills Revolution.* London, CBI.
Children Act (1989). London, HMSO.
Clare, M. (1990). *Developing Self Advocacy Skills.* London, FEU/EMFEC.
Department of Employment (1990). *Training Credits for Young People.* London, DE.
DES (24/91/NS). *Transition from School to Further Education for Students with Learning Difficulties* – Autumn 1989 – Spring 1990. London, DES.
Disabled Persons (Services, Consultation and Representation) Act (1986). London, HMSO.
Education Act (1981). London, HMSO.
Education Reform Act (1988). London, HMSO.
Evans, J., Everard, B., Friend, J., Glaser, A., Norwich, B. and Welton, J. (1989). *Decision Making for Special Educational Needs: An Inter-Service Resource Pack.* Loughborough, Techmedia Limited.
FEU (1986). *Transition to Adulthood.* London, FEU.
FEU (1987a). *Quality in NAFE.* London, FEU.
FEU (1987b). *Adults with Special Needs.* London, FEU.
FEU (1987c). *Planning Staff Development.* London, FEU.
FEU (1988a). *Occasional Paper. No. 6 Care and Education in the Community.* London, FEU.

FEU (1988b). *Planning the Curriculum*. London, FEU.
FEU (1988c). *Flexible Learning Opportunities and Special Educational Needs*. London, FEU.
FEU (1989a). *The Strategic Planning of Further Education*. London, FEU.
FEU (1989b). *Occasional Paper No. 7 Descriptions, Definitions and Directions*. London, FEU.
FEU (1989c). *Working Together? (A Series of Studies)*. London, FEU.
FEU (1989d). *Implementation of a Competence Based Curriculum*. London, FEU.
FEU (1989e). *Towards a Framework for Curriculum Entitlement*. London, FEU.
FEU (1989f). *Towards an Educational Audit*. London, FEU.
FEU (1989g). *The Youth Work Curriculum*. London, FEU.
FEU (1990a). *National Vocational Qualifications and Learners with Special Needs*. London, FEU.
FEU (1990b). *Bulletin -- The Core Skills*. London, FEU.
FEU (1990c). *Planning FE. Equal Opportunities for People with Disabilities and Special Educational Needs*. London, FEU.
FEU (1990d). *Individuality in Learning*. London, FEU.
FEU/NFER (1982). *From Coping to Confidence*. London, FEU/NFER.
FEU/Pickup (1988). *Quality Assurance*. London, FEU.
FEU/Training Agency/SKILL (1989). *Learning Support - A Staff Development Resource Pack*. London, FEU.
Fish, J. (1989). *What is Special Education?* Milton Keynes, Open University Press.
Gerry, M. (1989). *From School to Work in Genoa*. Unpublished report. Paris, OECD.
Goacher, B., Evans, J., Welton, J. and Weddell, K. (1988). *Policy and Provision for Special Educational Needs: Implementing the 1981 Education Act*. London, Cassell.
Hardman, M. (1988). *Supported Employment*. Unpublished report. Paris, OECD.
HMSO (1978). *Special Educational Needs* (The Warnock Report) Cmnd 7212. London, HMSO.
ILEA (1985). *Educational Opportunities for All?* London, ILEA.
Jowett, S., Hegarty, S. and Moses, D. (1988). *Joining Forces: A Study of Links between Ordinary and Special Schools*. Slough, NFER/Nelson.
MENCAP (1989). *Why Stop at 19?* London, MENCAP.
National Assistance Act (1948). London, HMSO.
National Health Service and Community Care Act (1990). London, HMSO.
NROVA (1990). *School and College Based Records of Achievement*. NVQ Research and Development Report, No. 8. London, NCVQ.
OECD (1986). *Young People with Handicaps - The Road to Adulthood*. Paris, OECD.
OECD (1987). *Active Life for Young People with Disabilities*. Paris, OECD.
OECD (1988). *Disabled Youth - The Right to Adult Status*. Paris, OECD.
OECD (1990). *Labour Market Policies for the 1990's*. Paris, OECD.
OECD (1991). *Disabled Youth: From School to Work*. Paris, OECD.

Open University (1986). *Mental Handicap. Patterns for Living*. Multi-media study Pack, P555. Open University, Learning Materials Service Office.

RNIB (1989). *Vocational College in Association with Loughborough*. London, RNIB.

Sailor, W., Anderson, D. L., Halvorsen, Ed. D., Doering, K., Filller, J. and Goetz, L. (1989). *The Local Comprehensive School*. Baltimore, USA, Paul H. Brookes.

Social Security Act (1988). London, HMSO.

SKILL (1990). *The Leicester Compact and Special Schools Involvement*. November, Educare.

Stevenson College (1991). *Evaluation Report. A Special Assessment and Training*. Edinburgh, Stevenson College.

Stowell (1987). *Catching Up*. Belfast, National Bureau for Handicapped Students.

The Americans with Disabilities Act (1990). Fact Sheet. President's Committee on Employment for People with Disabilities.

TEED (1990). *The Management of Quality BS 5750 and Beyond*. Sheffield, TEED.

Vincent, A. T. (1989). *New Technology, Disability and Special Educational Needs*. Coventry, Empathy Ltd, Hereward College.

Warburton, R. W. (1990). *Developing Services for Disabled People*. London, Department of Health.

Wehman, P., Moon, M. S., Everson, J. M., Wood, W. and Barcus, J. M. (1988). *Transition from School to Work*. Baltimore, USA, Paul H. Brookes.

Index